WAGNER

THE CONCERTGOER'S COMPANIONS
SERIES EDITOR ALEC HYATT KING

BACH by Alec Robertson
BEETHOVEN by Rosemary Hughes
BRAHMS by Kathleen Dale
CHOPIN by Derek Melville
HANDEL by Charles Cudworth
HAYDN by Brian Redfern
MOZART by Alec Hyatt King
WAGNER by Robert Anderson

WAGNER

A biography, with a survey of
books, editions and recordings

by

ROBERT ANDERSON

CLIVE BINGLEY
LONDON

LINNET BOOKS
HAMDEN · CONN

FIRST PUBLISHED 1980 BY CLIVE BINGLEY LTD
1-19 NEW OXFORD STREET LONDON WC1
SIMULTANEOUSLY PUBLISHED IN THE USA BY LINNET BOOKS
AN IMPRINT OF THE SHOE STRING PRESS INC
995 SHERMAN AVENUE HAMDEN CONNECTICUT 06514
SET IN 12 ON 13 POINT ALDINE ROMAN BY ALLSET
AND PRINTED AND BOUND IN THE UK BY
REDWOOD BURN LTD OF TROWBRIDGE AND ESHER
BINGLEY ISBN: 0-85157-279-0
LINNET ISBN: 0-208-01677-5

Library of Congress Cataloging in Publication Data

Anderson, Robert, 1927-
  Wagner : a biography.

  (The concertgoer's companions)
  Includes index.
  1. Wagner, Richard, 1813-1883.   2. Wagner, Richard,
1813-1883—Bibliography.   3. Wagner, Richard, 1813-
1883—Discography.   4. Composers—Germany—Biography.
ML410.W1A599   782.1'092'4 [B]   80-374
ISBN 0-208-01677-5 (Linnet)

Contents

Wagner's life   9

Books in English about Wagner   76

Editions of Wagner's music   110

Selected recordings of Wagner's music   126

Index   145

For Roger Oliver, librarian and friend, whose resources produced books, scores, and discs beyond expectation

Gratitude is due for encouragement and many courtesies to Patricia Hill and T G H James, as to Raymond Hounslow of the Chiswick District Library, Eric Hughes of the British Institute of Recorded Sound, and John Mitchell of Discurio; their assistance has been much appreciated.

Wagner's Life

In the summer of 1869 a slow train to Lucerne brought three French devotees on a visit to Richard Wagner and Cosima von Bülow. They shared the enthusiasm of priests for the Wagnerian cause, the fanaticism of martyrs. They were Count Villiers de l'Isle Adam, grand master of the knights of Malta and claimant to the Greek throne; Catulle Mendès, poet and future author of *Le roi vierge*, a novel banned in Bavaria because of its treatment under thin disguise of king Ludwig II; and Judith Gautier, then Mendès's wife, known to the Wagners as 'the hurricane'. During their discussions *en route* they set Wagner above Homer, Aeschylus, Dante, Goethe, Beethoven, and Shakespeare.

Wagner himself claimed he was fatal to the Napoleons. By the end of 1812 Napoleon I was in Paris after the retreat from Moscow. In April 1813 he had a new army and was making for Leipzig. In early May he won the battle of Lützen; on May 20 and 21 he fought indecisively at Bautzen; on May 22 in Leipzig Wilhelm Richard Wagner was born. According to Ludwig Geyer, friend of Wagner's legal father Friedrich and soon to be the boy's step-father, Napoleon had promised to make Saxony a paradise: the inhabitants were already reduced to their shirts and the state of ultimate innocence seemed near enough. But Napoleon left Saxony after losing the battle of Leipzig in mid-October, and on November 23 Friedrich Wagner died of typhus, indirectly a war casualty.

PARENTAGE AND CHILDHOOD

Wagner's parentage has caused controversy. His mother, Johanna Rosina Pätz, brought up by a baker from Weissenfels, a diminutive and eccentric woman who wore nine caps to keep her head warm, was strongly religious and made up with ready wit for defects in education. A slight embarrassment about her origins and hints of an aristocratic protector have suggested her father may have been Prince Constantine of Sachsen-Weimar, a young man as musical as he was wild. In the case of Friedrich Wagner, police actuary descended from a line of cantors, schoolmasters and tax-collectors, devotee of the theatre and its actresses, an exotic character according to E T A Hoffmann and in his cups 'un poco exaltato', there is a suspicion Ludwig Geyer may have supplanted him to beget Richard. Wagner thought so in 1869 when instructing Friedrich Nietzsche to affix a 'vulture' crest to the first printing of *Mein Leben*, part 1 (Geier is the German for vulture); later he rejected the idea, though his own son Siegfried occasionally reminded him of Geyer. Perhaps he summed up the matter when offered in 1881 the purchase of his birth house: 'I can't be born again'.

Geyer became Wagner's stepfather in August 1814, Johanna having been a widow less than the ten months demanded by Saxon law. Wagner's stepsister Cäcilie was born the following February. A man of sensitive disposition, weak constitution and many parts, Geyer intrigued Wagner. He died when the boy was only eight; but he had sung tenor for Weber, wrote a play, *The slaughter of the innocents*, that interested Goethe, and painted portraits for the royal houses of Bavaria, Saxony and Prussia. He called his high-spirited stepson 'the Cossack' and said it was a daily occurrence for Richard to leave the seat of his pants on a hedge. When dying, he wondered, on the strength of a couple of piano pieces played by Richard, whether the boy might be a musician.

Wagner was a sickly child and avid for feminine sympathy, which he seldom got from his mother and five sisters amid the rough and tumble of a large family. He was fascinated by his sisters' dresses and kept rabbits in a chest of drawers. Inanimate objects such as beer bottles scared him, or pieces of furniture imagined into hostile life. He filched coins from the box of his favourite sister Rosalie, sold a volume of Schiller to buy cream puffs, and was so soft-hearted he was dubbed Bailiff Scrambled Eggs. To get out of a scrape at school he told such thumping lies the masters commended his imagination; at home he made cardboard clouds and was cross when they wouldn't float from the backs of chairs. He claimed to have grown up in wildest anarchy.

After Geyer's death in September 1821, Richard was briefly cared for by his stepfather's younger brother. The following summer he stayed in the splendid Leipzig house where his uncle Adolf Wagner lived, a literary figure of distinction as author of four comedies and a novel, translator of Byron and Gozzi, commentator on Caesar and Euripides, and in his last year editor of Robert Burns. Wagner later remembered reading *Paradise and the Peri* and *Manfred* in a window where hyacinths stood, and in 1869 was still dipping pleasurably into his uncle's books on Dante and Erasmus. As schoolboy he was dragged through Cornelius Nepos, translated Plutarch 'with incredible hardship', attempted some books of the *Odyssey*, was enchanted by Greek myths, wrote with a friend ecstatic sacred poems, mourned a school-fellow in elaborate but effective verse, was so taken by the demonic intensity of Shakespeare he searched for mystic qualities in Falstaff, and devised for a spectre in his own first tragedy the telling line, 'Touch me not! This nose of mine must fall to dust should mortal seize it'.

Temperamentally he made always for the heart of a subject. He was bewitched by Weber's *Freischütz* overture; therefore he must play the piano, not by means of scales and arpeggios, but by fumbling attempts at the overture itself. He wanted to write a quartet before knowing how the viola clef worked. In 1828 Beethoven's *Egmont* music was a revelation; so his own tragedy *Leubald und Adelaide* must have a similar setting. That year he entered the school of St Nicholas, Leipzig, where he had bad marks for conduct, industry, and progress. The lessons that appealed were gained from proof work on Becker's *Universal History* for his brother-in-law Friedrich Brockhaus, during which he immersed himself in the Middle Ages and the French revolution. In 1830 there was again revolution in Paris, with Lafayette once more astride the streets; there were demonstrations in Leipzig, with Wagner on guard at a city gate and at the Brockhaus printing works. His school days ended at St Thomas's Leipzig. Lacking proper leaving certificates, he enrolled as a music student at the university.

STUDIOSUS MUSICAE

Wagner's first surviving letter dates from October 1830: he wishes to interest the publisher Schott in a piano arrangement he is making of the Choral Symphony. Wagner claimed to have been swept into a musical career just before his sixteenth birthday when he heard Wilhelmine Schröder-Devrient as Beethoven's Leonora. He never forgot the dramatic power of her acting. Discipline came to his musical studies in 1831 with a course of composition under Theodor Weinlig, a successor of Bach's at St Thomas's. Among the results were an opus 1 piano sonata published by Breitkopf & Härtel, a D minor overture owing much to Beethoven's *Coriolan*, a C major overture he failed to recognise when it was played for his sixtieth birthday, and the C major symphony of 1832, performed at the Leipzig Gewandhaus the following year and noticed as far afield as the London *Harmonicon*. As university student Wagner evaded three duels (one opponent lapsed from a severed artery, another had to fight in Jena, the third was laid up after a brothel brawl). He also gambled dangerously but successfully with his mother's pension and suffered exalted agonies at the fall of Warsaw in 1831.

A Vienna obsessed with Hérold's *Zampa* and Strauss waltzes detained him briefly in the summer of 1832 on his way to the estate of Count Pachta near Prague, where he fell in love with the illegitimate black-eyed Jenny, went hunting and identified himself with the dying hare, and began a libretto for his first operatic venture, *Die Hochzeit*. This 'night piece of blackest colouring' was abandoned after the composition of three numbers, largely through the mockery of his sister Rosalie. But it was she who urged him to persevere with *Die Feen*, an opera of redemption based on Gozzi already hinting at the mature Wagner. 'You have only to dare, dear brother', she said.

A PROVINCIAL BATON

Richard's eldest brother Albert, a tenor at the Jesuit stronghold of Würzburg, outside Saxony, was married to a highly-rouged and pock-marked gorgon whom Wagner detested. But to avoid military service and earn money while writing *Die Feen* Wagner took a job there as chorus master. He had the chance to rehearse such operatic favourites of the day as Meyerbeer's *Robert the devil*, Marschner's *Hans Heiling* and *Der Vampyr* (for which he wrote an extended conclusion to Aubry's Act 3 aria). Marschner and Weber were the main influences on *Die Feen*, which was completed on 6 January 1834.

He hoped *Die Feen* might be staged in Leipzig, where Rosalie was a respected actress but where the director's taste was dominated by regret that Bach had never written an opera. There was some talk of a production with oriental turbans and caftans; Wagner characteristically insisted on a northern setting; and neither occurred. Heinrich Laube, Wagnerian friend and enemy, described him at the time as 'bursting with self-confidence', knowing already he could function as musician only when also his own dramatist. Yet there was uncertainty of direction. Was not the German instrumental tradition 'too intellectual and much too learned' for opera? Thus he argued in his first essay (1834), *On German opera*, castigated in 1878 as 'shameless' on the grounds that he then knew no Gluck, and Weber's *Euryanthe* only from a bad performance. Again it was Schröder-Devrient's influence, this time as the dying Romeo in Bellini's *I Montecchi ed i Capuleti*, that was decisive. 'To the devil with classical music' was his conclusion; *Das Liebesverbot*, based on Shakespeare's *Measure for Measure*, relying for its music mainly on Auber and Bellini, was the result.

Looking back with his second wife Cosima on his early career Wagner said it was the existence of the two operas that alone convinced him of its reality. Yet it was also the time he took a wife. It may have been hard to credit the absurdities of the Bethmann troupe he joined in 1834 and lampooned in a one-act sketch he wrote in 1868 with such characters as Barnabas Kühlewind the prompter, Kaspar Schreiblich a depraved student, and Napoleon Baldachin impersonator of heroes. Yet in a skyblue dress coat and cuffs as big as clouds it was heaven to be conducting, particularly when the first opera was Mozart and *Don Giovanni*. This was in Bad Lauchstädt, where Wagner met Minna Planer, actress member of the company, already mother of the eight-year old Natalie (who was always given out as a sister). He was overwhelmed by her beauty and poise, by her affectionate sympathy during one of the attacks of bacterial skin disease that plagued him. They became engaged in February 1835. He once pointed out to Cosima the Magdeburg apartment where they lived: 'Up there we kept our brilliant household with love, the poodle, and the summonses for debt'.

While still employed by Bethmann at Magdeburg in 1835, Wagner toured for singers. One evening he came to Bayreuth, gloriously lit by the evening sun; at Nuremberg he witnessed a near-riot which ended instantly one of the combatants was knocked out; at Frankfurt he pawned a snuff-box and signet ring given by his friend Theodor Apel and started diary jottings in his Red Book (eventually the basis of *Mein Leben*). The Magdeburg company collapsed in financial ruin, but not before *Das Liebesverbot* had received a nightmare first performance on 29 March 1836, with singers making up for defective memory by inserting snatches of other operas, and Wagner's creditors, his 'accursed rabble of Jews', baulked of the success his optimism had foretold. From the heights of *Parsifal, Das*

14

Liebesverbot seemed to Wagner 'horrible, hideous, loathsome', with only hail and thunder in the overture. But it was well orchestrated: 'I knew about that in my mother's womb'. The relationship with Minna was often stormy. Wagner was unemployed and irascible, Minna reduced to wearisome nagging. Yet when she took work in Berlin, Wagner's passionate bombardment of daily letters apparently wrenched from the bottom of his soul wore down her resistance. Laube counselled books rather than marriage; but on 24 November 1836 the wedding took place before a frivolous theatre congregation in Königsberg. They had quarrelled when visiting the clergyman. Wagner maintained he had married from jealousy; Minna characterised him at the time as 'a poor, forlorn, unknown conductor out of a job'. During the service Wagner had to be nudged for the ring; he concentrated only when the clergyman mentioned a friend who would undoubtedly help them, and his interest lapsed when this turned out to be Jesus. Schröder-Devrient now called him 'the marriage cripple'. Yet in 1881, with Minna dead already fifteen years, memories of her beauty lingered, and he told Cosima his instinct had been sound: 'All follies were cut off from me, and I thought only of work'.

As composer and dramatist Wagner was marking time. In 1835 he had composed an overture to Theodor Apel's play *Columbus* (straight from Mendelssohn's *Calm sea and prosperous voyage*, he thought later); the following year the *Polonia* overture, tribute to the Polish exiles he had known in Leipzig; and in 1837 what he misspelt as a *Rule Brittania* overture, homage to England as opponent of the Holy Alliance. He sketched *Die hohe Braut*, a draft audaciously and pointlessly sent to Scribe for versification into French, and *Die glückliche Bärenfamilie,* based on the *1001 Nights*, featuring an acrobatic bear called Richard and needing the lightest French touch for its setting.

A brief period from April 1837 as music director at Königsberg prepared for Wagner's last provincial appointment, which he took up at Riga in August. Depressed by much of the repertoire (his song *Der Tannenbaum* was written in E flat minor, the Lithuanian key of 'fir-tree melancholy'), but intrigued by the novel design of the theatre, which provided some ideas for Bayreuth, Wagner now turned his thoughts to Paris, operatic capital of the world. His engine of assault should be *Rienzi*, five-act metropolitan opera on Bulwer Lytton's novel that he had been pondering since summer 1837. Heinrich Dorn, Wagner's successor at Riga, has left a description of early *Rienzi* sessions: 'The wires of the piano would fly asunder like spray before the wind, so that the composer at last could bring out nothing but a flail-like rattle, accompanied by the pleasing jangle of metal snakes as they writhed on the keyboard'.

Meanwhile there had been mounting Minna problems, with desertion and threats of divorce. In October 1837 she returned and Wagner jotted in his Red Book 'Repentance'. While he sat at his Riga window puffing a pipe, wearing dressing gown and Turkish fez, the Paris vision clarified: Scribe should translate his texts; Meyerbeer, operatic favourite of the day, should underpin his fame; and the debt mountain, which threatened to topple and extinguish him, would be bypassed. Lacking passports (unavailable lest he abscond), the Wagners began a nightmare flight from Riga in July 1839. There was vigil in a smugglers' den, crossing of a ditch at the Russian frontier under the eye of Cossack guards, overturn of a waggon taking them to the Prussian port of Pillau, and boarding of the tiny ship Thetis under cloak of darkness. During a storm-racked journey that lasted three times the scheduled eight days, the Thetis lost her figurehead in the Kategat. Wagner, lying prostrate on top of the ship's brandy supply, had to keep his Newfoundland dog Robber off a furtively tippling sailor. It was compensation perhaps to see Hamlet's Elsinore and hear pre-echoes of *Der fliegende Holländer (The Flying Dutchman)* as the sailors shouted within the resounding walls of a Norwegian fjord.

On 12 August 1839 the Wagners reached London and stayed long enough to deplore the cost of living. They lodged

16

in the City at the Hoop and Horseshoe, Queen Street, then in Soho at the King's Arms, Old Compton Street. Robber was unnerved and disappeared for two hours. When reunited, they made their first railway journey, to Gravesend Park; and Wagner thought the English poetical for using Nelson's Dreadnought at Greenwich as a home for old sailors (he dropped Schröder-Devrient's snuff-box over the side). He is said to have stood long and abstracted before Shakespeare's statue in Westminster Abbey. He failed to find Sir George Smart or Bulwer Lytton; instead he heard Wellington in the Lords and a 'stiff and unnatural' Bishop of London on the anti-slavery bill. On August 20 they left for Boulogne.

Female Jewish contacts on the boat furnished an introduction to Meyerbeer, who happened to be in Boulogne at the time. He was sufficiently impressed with what he heard and saw of *Rienzi* (Acts 1 and 2 were all but complete) to offer assistance for the conquest of Paris and suavely to admire Wagner's hand-writing. Yet Meyerbeer, composer of a ballet of nuns in *Robert the devil*, may have failed to appreciate the deadly integrity that was at the heart of Wagner.

THE PARISIAN ASPIRANT

Certainly Paris failed to fall; nor did Meyerbeer's letters prevent a courteous lack of interest from the director of the Opéra, the bankruptcy of the Théâtre de la Renaissance the moment it accepted *Das Liebesverbot*, and the neglect of fashionable singers to take up the French songs Wagner composed for aristocratic drawing rooms. At the end of 1840 he wrote to Schumann: 'I've been almost a year and a half in Paris and am doing splendidly, for I've not yet starved to death'. But he may already have been in a debtors' prison; though letters ostensibly from Minna to Theodor Apel mentioning jail were possibly dramatising a bad situation the more effectively to urge funds (which Apel gave). How else did Wagner survive? By pawning wedding presents, Minna's theatre wardrobe, rings and trinkets; by soliciting contributions from his brother-in-law Avenarius (Cäcilie's husband),

17

from a former suitor of the now dead Rosalie's, and Leipzig relatives; by hack arrangements of such operas as Donizetti's *La favorita* for the publisher Maurice Schlesinger; and by high-spirited journalism that enshrined his 'impassioned tangle of ideas' in a limpid prose suggesting it was good to be young and hungry in Paris.

Nothing is more amusing in the Paris writings than Wagner's description of the ageing tenor Rubini masterfully simpering an inaudible top B flat, received the more rapturously the less it could be heard; or the librettist Eugène Scribe at his 10 a.m. cocoa in elegant silk dressing gown, eyeing all the authors and composers of Paris with a fleeting smile, impartially concocting plots for them or from them. Nothing is more moving than *A pilgrimage to Beethoven*, where Wagner's youthful veneration spills over in mockery of an English lion hunter and has the deaf master grappling with the elements of Wagnerian theory. Indeed under the influence of Paris, which exuded 'the pestilential breath of a modern Babylon', Wagner was thoughtful of his German origin. At the end of 1839 he had heard the three instrumental movements of the Ninth Symphony at the Conservatoire under Habeneck and had written the first version of his *Faust* overture as result. On 19 November 1840 *Rienzi*, the Parisian grand opera owing much to Spontini, Meyerbeer and Auber, was complete. But already that summer Wagner had prepared for audition part of *Der fliegende Holländer,* the earliest of his operas he would countenance for Bayreuth, his sombre mingling of Odysseus and the wandering Jew.

At a first meeting in the Louvre the painter Friedrich Pecht thought Wagner almost too good-looking, too neat. But he came to appreciate the magic of his temperament, 'his bubbling vitality and winning presence, together with his enormous force of will'. Even in fiercest rage or maddest hilarity he somehow preserved for Pecht a charm and dignity: the artist was at one with the man. Other Parisian friends were Gottfried Anders, employee in the music section of the Bibliothèque Nationale with whom Wagner planned but never wrote a two-volume book on Beethoven; Samuel Lehrs, a consumptive Jew and classical scholar who called himself Siegfried when taking up Christianity; and Ernst Benedikt Kietz, a portrait painter so slow most of his sitters had departed from Paris or life before he finished a picture.

Wagner met in Paris both Berlioz and Liszt. In time Liszt became a major prop to Wagner's life and art; for the moment an impoverished young man saw only the salon idol, elegant equally before his mirror and at the piano, capable of desecrating a recital in aid of a Beethoven statue with encore fantasia on *Robert the devil*. Between the impulsive Wagner and world-weary, proud Berlioz there was little ease; but the music, particularly *Roméo et Juliette* and the *Symphonie funèbre et triomphale*, taught its lesson.

By the end of June 1841 Wagner's sufferings, the patience of his friends, and Minna's care-worn loyalty had their reward: *Rienzi* was accepted at the Dresden Court Theatre, the intendant Baron von Lüttichau and his committee having been much taken with it. Before leaving Paris in April 1842 Wagner made sketches for two further operatic projects, the *Saracen woman*, and the *Mines of Falun*. More significantly, reports of the Königsberg German Society supplied by Lehrs touched on the Wartburg singing contest and the story of Lohengrin. Kietz gave Wagner snuff and a five-franc piece as parting gift, and Minna wept most of the way to Germany. Wagner tried to console her, but after a snuffle she could only ask, 'May I cry again now?' Once in the fatherland Wagner turned a deep blue gaze on the river Rhine, which he had not seen before; he was moved too by the castle on the Wartburg and had pleasure enough to endure the vile weather and jostling Jews of the Leipzig fair.

Rienzi rehearsals began in August. Wagner's impatience filled the four-month gap with tireless talk at the silent Schumann; propaganda for the *Dutchman* in Berlin; a summer holiday sketching *Tannhäuser* on the highest peak in the neighbourhood with Minna and his mother; and first acquaintance with his future Elisabeth, the fifteen-year old

19

adopted daughter of his brother Albert. *Rienzi* was shrewdly calculated for Dresden success. The tenor Tichatschek, who preferred shooting to rehearsing, was enamoured of himself as silver-clad tribune of the people; Schröder-Devrient could deploy all her dramatic skill in a fiery death within the collapsing Capitol; only Wagner, kept going during the preparations by his Papal legate (who denounced him to the police in 1849) seemed incredulous and almost bemused both by the length of his opera and its triumph on 20 October 1842. He was too tired to notice the laurel wreath Minna had put in his bed.

DRESDEN ACCEPTED AND REJECTED

On the morrow Wagner could think of nothing but cuts in the work; though he also wrote to the Avenariuses in Paris that '*Never*, as they all assure me, has any opera been received for the first time in Dresden with such enthusiasm as my *Rienzi*'. Within a month Joseph Rastrelli, the Dresden music director, died, and at the beginning of 1843 Wagner was the victim of his success: *Der fliegende Holländer* was given on January 2, to some bewilderment because of its brooding strangeness, its lack of pageantry and absence of obvious effect; he was appointed as second kapellmeister equal to Reissiger and had the first of his four meetings with king Friedrich Augustus; and at the beginning of February Laube's *Die elegante Welt* published in two instalments his *Autobiographical sketch*, succinct summary of his career to that point, with characteristic unguarded words on Berlioz. At thirty he felt he was settling down, furnished himself with broad hints of luxury, and built up the first of the wide-ranging book collections he so passionately needed and cherished. He was also plagued by scarce-remembered creditors and threats of prosecution.

In July *Das Liebesmahl der Apostel* was given in the Dresden Frauenkirche. In later years Wagner mocked its dearth of inspiration and the theatrical descent of the Holy Ghost; for the moment he noted that this work for

20

multitudinous male voices made a surprisingly feeble effect. During the summer he began the composition of *Tannhäuser*, completed on 13 April 1845, himself making the vocal score and ensuring financial collapse by having the full score lithographed for five hundred thalers. There was a Dresden story that the printer C F Meser had to retreat one floor nearer the garret every time he embarked on a Wagner score. Nor was *Tannhäuser*, when it came to performance on 19 October 1845, more rewarding in the Dresden theatre than to Wagner's finances. Again the public was puzzled, and Wagner tinkered with the ending. Von Lüttichau wondered why Tannhäuser should not receive absolution in Rome and marry Elisabeth. Wagner was troubled by doubts, felt an overpowering artistic loneliness, and seemed to himself 'a madman who speaks only to the wind'.

Already in the summer of 1845, when under doctor's orders and taking a cure at Marienbad, Wagner was restlessly shaping his future. He read about Hans Sachs and the rules of the Mastersingers, writing the complete prose sketch for a projected comic opera; he devoured Wolfram von Eschenbach's *Parzival* and the anonymous Lohengrin epic so that by early August he had ready a prose sketch for *Lohengrin* too. Creative zest and pride in the single-mindedness with which he had campaigned for the return of Weber's remains from Moorfields in December 1844 were set against a Dresden background less and less congenial. There was early aggravation from the orchestral leader Lipinski, who led mainly by being ahead of the other violins; there were two 'dying violas', symbol that orchestral staffing was awry; the repertoire was too large to develop any sense of style; court hierarchy was irksome; and most urgent of all were the debts, piled up through reliance on friends including Schröder-Devrient, who helped generously but whose latest lover insisted also on managing her finances, and the Dresden doctor Anton Pusinelli, who put at Wagner's disposal 'an unshakable great heart, through which he understood everything'. By August 1846, with ruin imminent, Wagner had to turn to Lüttichau for a loan from the pension fund of three and a half years' salary. His finances became the talk of Dresden.

A December 1845 scheme to launch *Tannhäuser* in Berlin came to nothing; to secure merely a dedication to the King of Prussia he would have had to arrange the airs for military band so that they could be heard at the changing of the guard. In November the *Lohengrin* poem had been read by Wagner to a group including the musicians Schumann and Hiller, the architect Semper, the painters Schnorr von Carolsfeld and Pecht. He began composition with Act 3, reverting to Acts 1 and 2 and finally the prelude, which was drafted by the end of July 1846. Scoring was ended on 28 April 1848. The main Dresden projects during work on *Lohengrin* were the Beethoven Ninth Symphony performed on Palm Sunday 1846 (Gade thought it was worth the journey just to hear the finale recitatives) and furnished by Wagner with extracts from Goethe's *Faust* as programme commentary; and Gluck's *Iphigeneia in Aulis*, reworked by Wagner to get as close as possible to the Euripides play and opening on 22 February 1847 (Schumann thought Wagner's arrangement an impertinence). That summer Wagner was immersed in Aeschylus and Aristophanes, forging immediately ahead to consider the Norse and German sagas in the light of the ancient world.

In January 1848 Wagner's mother died. She had seen his success but probably knew nothing of his increasing coolness towards the Dresden theatre. He attended policy meetings rarely, emerging like a 'sulking Achilles' to debate with supreme irrelevance the merits of Gluck and Piccinni during casting talks. His mind was seething with other matters. Already the previous November he had bewailed the political situation: 'Here is a barrier to break through, and the means is called Revolution!' August Röckel, son of Beethoven's Florestan in 1806 and now musical director at Dresden, brought Wagner news of the Paris uprising in February while he was conducting Flotow's *Martha*. The Wagners' parrot Papo could whistle tunes from *Rienzi*; it would also squawk

'Richard! Freedom!'. Wagner wrote a poem to celebrate revolts in Vienna, sent a political agenda to Professor Wigard, Saxon representative of the national assembly in Frankfurt, and became friendly with acknowledged revolutionaries.

Wagner pursued his meditations 'perched on a high branch of a tree, or on the neck of the Neptune which was the central figure of a large group of statuary in the middle of an old fountain'. A focus of the Dresden agitators was Michael Bakunin, intimate at the time of Karl Marx but later hostile to his 'official democracy and red bureaucracy'. Apparently on an impulse, Wagner the court official read out to the Vaterlandsverein a revolutionary prepared text lambasting court administration and urging Friedrich Augustus 'the worthiest, noblest king' to speak out and declare Saxony a free state.

In April 1849 Wagner wrote an article for Röckel's paper the *Volksblätter,* hymning 'the sublime goddess Revolution'. According to Cosima's diary, Minna's fears were silenced by telling her the movement could not fail and he would probably be made secretary of the provisional government. He also maintained he would never have conceived *The Ring* without such political upheaval. The previous summer had indeed been fruitful, with an essay on the Wibelungs and a dramatic sketch on Friedrich Barbarossa. Ashton Ellis thus sums up the Wibelung argument: 'the Hoard was also the Grail, and Frederick was Siegfried, and Siegfried was Baldur, and Baldur was Christ'. In 1871 Wagner thumbed through the essay again and was glad to see he had talked less nonsense than he feared. During November 1848 *Siegfrieds Tod,* first version of the *Götterdämmerung* poem, was written in the 'Stabreim stammer', the alliterative verse so suited to Wagner's purpose and such a stumbling block at the time to friends and foes.

Beethoven's Ninth was again done by Wagner on Palm Sunday 1849. At a rehearsal Bakunin affirmed that should all other music go up in the flames of the conflagration to come, that symphony must be rescued. A month later Joy's divine sparks were flying in the streets of Dresden. Prussian troops were ready to assist the Saxon government, and there was news of their approach on May 2. Bakunin and his cigar were among the barricades, which the architect Semper strengthened; Wagner distributed posters to the soldiers asking whether their loyalty was with the citizens or the Prussians. Some say he purchased hand grenades and took guns from Tichatschek's house; certainly he was on the tower of the Kreuzkirche, intoxicated by the 'combination of the bells and cannon', watching for troop movements outside the city, throwing messages tied to stones, discussing with Professor Thum philosophic attitudes in the ancient world and Christianity. When a week had passed and the fires of rebellion were low, he left the city with Bakunin and others. At Freiburg they separated. Bakunin and his companions were captured, condemned to death, and later given life sentences; Wagner was free, but a wanted man.

His niece Johanna, Elisabeth in *Tannhäuser*, wrote to Lüttichau expressing indignation at the rebels' ingratitude; his relative Heinrich Brockhaus took over Wagner's library as security for a debt that was never settled. Wagner himself was at Weimar, listening in at a *Tannhäuser* orchestral rehearsal and admiring the flexibility of Liszt's conducting, discussing with Princess Wittgenstein the *Jesus of Nazareth* play he had sketched earlier in the year, paying a first visit to the Wartburg he had brought to such dramatic life in *Tannhäuser*. His revolution, he felt, had been constructive; after some months he would doubtless return to Dresden and resume court duties. But Minna sent news of the warrant for his arrest. Even now he would not admit to Liszt he had acted foolishly. 'Richard! Freedom!' the parrot had said; and in after years Wagner felt the beginning of his Swiss exile was one of the two happiest moments in his life (the other followed the Paris *Tannhäuser*).

WANDERER AND THINKER

A piano teaching friend from Würzburg days, Alexander Müller, who had given Act 1 of *Der fliegende Holländer* and written an opera called *The flight to Switzerland*, was his first Zürich refuge. By the end of May Wagner had satisfied Liszt's urging that he should make for Paris. Equipped with a Swiss passport describing him as '36 years old; 5 ft 5½ inches high; hair brown, eyebrows brown, eyes blue; nose medium, mouth medium, chin round', and riding in a coach of which the wheels seemed to be playing 'Freude, schöner Götterfunken' from the Ninth Symphony, he reached Paris on June 2. He had a vague plan to get *Rienzi* performed and then write an opera specially for Paris. But there was cholera in the city; and Meyerbeer also, who asked whether he would now be composing exclusively for the barricades. After reading Proudhon on property and Lamartine's history of the Girondins, Wagner gave way to Parisian discouragement and he was back in Zürich on July 6.

The immediate Dresden legacy was personal loneliness, the need to sort out his revolutionary experience, and the slow-working implications of the Siegfried poem. Wagner now produced the first of those treatises that so appalled Princess Wittgenstein: 'Ne me parlez de ces grosses bêtises'. *Art and revolution* made onslaught on a society whose god was gold, recommending instead the two sublime teachers of mankind, Jesus the sufferer, Apollo who raised men to their joyous dignity. *The artwork of the future* became a dream of intellectual harmony based on a company of geniuses and made first use of the term 'Gesamtkunstwerk'. Professor Bischoff of Cologne replied with mockery of 'music of the future', a happy phrase that caused Wagner much suffering. In September Minna, aged by the loss of Dresden security, and threatening departure at the slightest sign of misbehaviour, arrived in Zürich with daughter, dog, and parrot.

Liszt and Minna still looked to a Paris success and Wagner worked out a prose sketch of *Wieland the Smith*, story of a cripple who eventually wings his way to freedom. Liszt

25

recommended also ballads and perhaps an oratorio text for himself on Byron's *Heaven and earth*. Before leaving for Paris at the beginning of February 1850, Wagner had an offer of joint financial help from a Dresden acquaintance, Julie Ritter, and the Laussot family of Bordeaux. Paris was haunted by Meyerbeer again, who depressed him with the current success of *Le prophète*, and by barrel organs. *Wieland* seemed impossible and, instead of returning to Zürich, Wagner took up an invitation to Bordeaux in mid-March. The saga of the next two months involved increasing affection for the young wife, Jessie Laussot, who was pianist enough to play the *Hammerklavier* sonata. There were plans for elopement to Greece or Asia Minor, letters to Minna about separation (she would get half his money), and collusion between Jessie's mother and Minna to frustrate Wagner's intention of committing adultery. In May Wagner visited Bordeaux to see the husband, who was now ready to shoot him but had sensibly removed the whole household to the country. Withdrawal of the financial offer on the Bordeaux side then followed. When the crisis was over, Minna wrote: 'I certainly will not and can *never* forget it'; Wagner confided to Theodor Uhlig, a serious young violinist in the Dresden orchestra, that he now had a brand-new wife, who had been through a fiery ordeal but would stand by him till death.

In the midst of the Jessie episode Wagner urged on Liszt the production of *Lohengrin*: 'To no one but you could I entrust the 'creation' of this opera; but to you I deliver it unconditionally'. Plans to give *Lohengrin* in Dresden had been abandoned at the end of 1848 when there was every reason for displeasure with Wagner. More and more the work came to symbolise for Wagner his withdrawal from a world that misunderstood him; Lohengrin's departure at the end of the opera seemed to him the essence of the matter. At Weimar, inadequately equipped with chorus and orchestra, Liszt launched the swan-knight among the Brabantines on 28 August 1850 as part of the Goethe birthday celebrations. Wagner, unable to be present, climbed the Rigi with Minna, whose heart was not up to the exertion, and he passed the evening watch in hand at The Swan in Lucerne.

SWISS NOTES AND NOTABLES
That same month Wagner made a start on the music of *Siegfrieds Tod*, setting fifty lines of the Norns' scene and twenty of the opening duet between Siegfried and Brünnhilde. For the moment the sketches were put aside and Wagner, goaded by an article Uhlig wrote on *Le prophète* and the question of 'Jewish taste', set about expressing 'his long repressed resentment about this Jew business', giving voice to the involuntary repulsion inspired in him by the nature and personality of the Jew, pin-pointing the Jewish pheno-menon as the evil conscience of modern civilisation. In the musical sphere there were attacks on the two wandering Jews, Mendelssohn and Meyerbeer, and the pamphlet, *Jewishness in music*, issued under the pseudonym K Freigedank, caused a 'dreadful commotion' and poisoned for ever Wagner's relations with the press, which he in any case despised as largely in the hands of Jews. On September 14 he outlined to Kietz in Paris the festival setting for which he would reserve his *magnum opus*, the Siegfried work.

A routine report on Wagner to the Dresden chief of police describes him as giving concerts in Zürich and couples his name with that of a notorious Jewish swindler and imposter. Wagner's Swiss conducting kept him modestly in the public eye and allowed him the chance to hear some of his own music. In the autumn of 1850 it also involved him with two young musicians he was anxious to launch, Karl Ritter, son of his Dresden patroness, and Hans von Bülow, whose mother thought Wagner's influence dangerous. To Bülow he wrote: 'Be brave, Hans, stand firm and all will come right'. Musically it did, and Bülow proved himself equally gifted as conductor and pianist pupil of Liszt's, describing Wagner to his mother as 'the noblest and kindest of men'; Ritter was a more complex case whose incompetence on the rostrum sometimes forced Wagner to take over at the Zürich theatre.

At the end of 1850 Wagner had planned his knottiest theoretical work, *Opera and drama,* written against a background of increasing obsession with water as a cure for all physical disorder. This was an article of faith held by the consumptive Uhlig; for Wagner, too, the properties of water became something of a mania, with baths in the morning, water to be drunk in bed, the wearing of a 'Neptune girdle'. *Opera and drama,* Wagner's signposting for himself of the difficult route to *The Ring,* occasionally baffled even the acolytes of Wahnfried. At Leipzig Wagner had attended lectures on aesthetics by a professor who excused his obscurity by saying the deepest problems of the mind could not be solved in the language of the mob. Wagner accepted this principle, and gave it freest expression in *Opera and drama.* Papo the parrot, who had learnt also to say 'Bad man! Poor Minna!' expired with the completion of the treatise in February 1851.

After *Lohengrin,* Wagner's main hopes for his Siegfried scheme were with Liszt, even when in April 1851 his dramatic instinct thrust him on to a *Young Siegfried* as companion piece to *Siegfried's Death.* The poem done, he wrote to Liszt in June 1851: 'I am *very* pleased with it, and anyhow it is what I was bound to do at the moment and the *best* that I have done up till now'. That summer he worked on *A communication to my friends,* urging that in his case 'to sever artist and man is as brainless as to divorce soul from body', tracing the progress of his art and thought. The end had to be rewritten in the autumn when Wagner, submitting to the treatment of a 'water Jew' at Albisbrunn in the company of incurables, and feebly trying to enliven dull evenings with desperate attempts at whist, came to the unalterable conclusion that the Siegfried scheme would consist of three operas and expository prologue. Uhlig in Dresden heard the news on October 12.

That summer he and Uhlig had tramped the Swiss mountains and explored William Tell country. The fantastic heights of Switzerland formed a proper backcloth for the development of *The Ring,* and Wagner's exuberance and cool head took him often to the lonely haunts of this other world. Looking back from 1874, he remembered a mountain disagreement that had been the source of Loge's mocking address to the Rhinemaidens; and in 1878 he recalled the Julier pass he had visited twenty-five years before: 'Where everything is silent, one thinks of the being which has power there'; he had in fact imagined the doomladen meeting of Wotan and Fricka in *Die Walküre*. At the top of the Siedelhorn in summer 1852 he had drunk champagne; at the crucial moment he couldn't think whom to toast.

In Zürich there was a growing circle of admirers. The fair-haired Wesendoncks get their first mention in Wagner's 'annals' of 1851. Otto, silk merchant with interests in America, had in fact attracted police attention as a democrat; Mathilde, his second wife, was thirteen years younger, became Wagner's amanuensis (inking in sketches) and 'muse'. George Herwegh, former revolutionary poet, now lazy as a 'foot gone to sleep', watched with detached amusement a Wagner 'curing himself thoroughly ill'. His wife Emma favoured Minna and thought Wagner a pocket edition of a man, calling him also 'this folio of vanity, heartlessness, and egotism' (but she had to marvel at his effect on the Zürich choir and orchestra). François Wille at Mariafeld 'had a horror of music', had accompanied the young Bismarck 'in studies, duels, debauches' (Newman's phrase), and became so impressed with Schopenhauer he made a yearly pilgrimage to see the Frankfurt philosopher; his wife Eliza had been acquainted with Wagner since Dresden days; 'she knows *everything* straight away', Otto Wesendonck wrote of her, and she was very likable 'in spite of her great ugliness'. The exiled Latin tutor to the Saxon princes despised the set-up: 'He has formed a little clique here of half a dozen people who make an idol of him, adore his arrogance and rudeness . . . and what is very useful, occasionally pay his debts'.

While busy with the *Young Siegfried* text in 1851, Wagner sketched music for the preludes to Acts 1 and 2 ('Fafner's repose' he called the latter). But it was the forging of the poem that now obsessed him, from the first prose sketch of *Rheingold*, originally in three acts, at the beginning of November 1851 to the reworking of *Young Siegfried* and *Siegfried's Death* in December 1852. Towards the end of the period Minna wrote to Johanna Wagner: 'He is more irritable than ever. His nerves bother him a lot, for which that horrid water cure that he tried a year ago and now carries on at home is mainly to blame'. Two hours' work was a terrible trial, from which he needed the rest of the day and night to recover. His solace was the Persian poet Hafez, depicter of 'laughing love'. The complete *Ring* poem was read at Mariafeld before Christmas, the ladies 'so much moved that they ventured no comment'; by the end of February 1853 Wagner had had it privately printed. Uhlig died before receiving his copy; it was sent instead to his son Siegfried (Wagner was the godfather).

Zürich friends underwrote a festival to celebrate Wagner's fortieth birthday in May 1853. The operas from *Rienzi* to *Lohengrin* were represented, a laurel wreath and silver goblet were handed over, and a poem, perhaps by Mathilde Wesendonck, was recited. 'I laid the whole festival at the feet of *one* beautiful woman', wrote Wagner; Mathilde received a polka and sonata movement for piano, the first compositions completed for five years. Wagner's prime object had been to hear some *Lohengrin*, particularly the prelude; as he explained to Liszt, 'the effect on myself was uncommonly moving and I had to pull myself together by force not to give way to it!'. And Liszt visited him in early July, enjoying his 'Valhalla days' with Wagner and thanking God for having created such a man, who 'wept and laughed and stormed with joy for at least a quarter of an hour at seeing me again'. They sang the Elsa-Lohengrin duet together and Liszt noted the house was furnished with some luxury.

THE RING MUSICIAN
Otto Wesendonck was indeed exercised how to order Wagner's finances and came to the conclusion Wagner could not be

trusted with money at all. Might it be given to Minna instead without intolerable affront? For the moment he financed an Italian holiday for Wagner, who at the end of August 1853 in Genoa saw the Mediterranean for the first time and then, wretchedly ill from eating too many ices, made for La Spezia, where half-unconscious he heard the rush and roar of the Rhine depths take shape as a surging chord of E flat. He was now ready for the music of *The Ring* and, as he later explained to Arrigo Boito, 'returned to the land of shadow to carry out that bulky work'. Composition was begun on November 1 after an excursion to Paris with Liszt and Princess Wittgenstein, during which he heard Meyerbeer's *Robert the devil*, the late Beethoven quartets in E flat and C sharp minor; and the three Liszt children, including the fifteen-year old Cosima, heard readings of *The Ring*.

The *Rheingold* composition was completed on 14 January 1854; soon afterwards Liszt performed a Nibelung opera by Heinrich Dorn, Wagner's Riga successor and now deadly enemy. Work on the *Rhinegold* full score (the fair copy was done on September 26) made Wagner marvel at the close thematic unity of the music, which revealed aspects of the poem he had not previously suspected. The theoretical writings were now no more than an abstract expression of the creative processes that had been shaping within him. The sketching of *Die Walküre* began on June 28. At the end of Act 1, on the recommendation of Herwegh, Wagner began to immerse himself in Schopenhauer, whose sombre philosophy gave him renewed insight into the character of Wotan and whose view of music as the fundamental art, the essential experience, an idea of the world in Plato's sense, helped to mature and release in Wagner the titanic musical forces that were to erupt in *Tristan*.

Schopenhauer's favourite music was Rossini and he felt no opera should last more than two hours. He thought Wagner more poet than composer, but annotated his copy of the *Ring* text with irreverent comments such as 'And high time too' when the *Walküre* Act 1 curtain came down on the twins' love-making; 'Wotan under the slipper' when Fricka gets the better of their altercation; 'The clouds play the principal role' when the Valkyries hold forth on their mountain peak. In December 1854 Wagner wrote to Liszt about Schopenhauer and *Tristan*, which possessed him with increasing urgency: 'Schopenhauer's main conception, the ultimate negation of the will to live, is terribly stern, but in it alone is salvation'. Wagner's negation expressed itself thus: 'I have planned in my mind a *Tristan und Isolde*, the simplest yet most full-blooded musical conception; then I will wrap myself in the 'black flag' which waves over its close and—die'.

But the *Ring* plans suggested to Wagner that if he lived to carry them out, he would have lived gloriously. He even toyed with Zürich as site for his festival theatre. In the spring of 1852 he tried out the *Dutchman* in Zürich, thinning the brass writing and modifying the accompaniment to such moments as Senta's Act 2 scream. That summer, as he told Uhlig, his travelling was done on the *Dutchman* honorarium: every day cost him one number of the opera, twenty francs. And in February 1855 there were Zürich *Tannhäuser* performances, modest enough with an image of the Virgin for eight francs, two tiger skins for three, and an Elisabeth who performed in kid gloves holding a fan. For Zürich, too, he revised in January 1855 the *Faust* overture of 1840, acting on suggestions from Liszt and his own new-found mastery.

'A simple and amiable-looking Englishman, Mr Anderson', had called on Wagner early in 1855: the Philharmonic Society of London wanted him to conduct a series of eight concerts. Needing money, he accepted with misgivings. The critics proved 'a band of vagabond Jews'; fogs obscured other impressions; London taste exacted Mendelssohn and programmes as dire in length as content. He lived near Regent's Park. Compensations included the exercise of a friend's dog, watching the sheep, feeding the ducks, and visiting the zoo (a lion's roars disturbed concentration during the scoring of *Walküre* Act 2). The reading of Dante suitably described his London 'Inferno'; he read also Indian sagas. The Queen and

Prince Albert attended the seventh concert, spoke warmly of the *Tannhäuser* overture and London chances for Wagner operas in Italian. He met also Malwida von Meysenbug, friend of Mazzini and Garibaldi, Liszt's 'mother superior of the order of free thought'; she was full of schemes for the perfection of the human race which the Schopenhauer-soaked Wagner found irrelevant. Berlioz was conducting in London too, and they came a little closer; Meyerbeer passed through, and they stayed poles apart.

After London Wagner returned to the death of his dog Peps, sorrowfully buried with basket and cushion, and to thirteen attacks of his skin disease lasting till the next summer; these he considered a legacy, along with a 'fine collection of latent rheums and catarrhs', of London's dankness. When ill he worked on the *Tristan* libretto, when feeling better proceeded with *Walküre*, the first two acts of which seemed to Liszt a miracle. Wagner himself had been troubled about the long Wotan-Brünnhilde scene in Act 2, wondering whether to cut it, yet recognising it as the spiritual core of *The Ring*. He thought the *Walküre* poem 'a superlative of sorrow, suffering and despair', was exhausted at the end of Act 3 in March 1856, yet convinced of the work's extraordinary beauty and aware that previously he had achieved nothing even approaching it.

For the writing of the *Walküre* score Mathilde Wesendonck had presented him with a gold pen of indestructible power; she also provided the new dog, Fips. The personal tangle now threatening the Wagners and Wesendoncks was less gossamer-webbed than before. Wagner would have liked to talk it over with Liszt; instead he sank himself in the prose sketch for a Buddhist subject, *The Victors*, and in a cure during which he 'indulged in tea to excess', was told by Dr Vaillant, 'Monsieur, vous n'êtes que nerveux', and convinced himself gradually back to health.

During the summer of 1856 his sister Klara, the only relative to visit him in Zürich, 'acted as a damper' on the frequent and bitter scenes he had with Minna. In spite of additional disturbance from a blacksmith opposite, Wagner launched on *Siegfried* Act 1 in September. Progress was interrupted by a visit from Liszt, who played the *Faust* and *Dante* symphonies but brought also the Princess Wittgenstein, that *monstrum per excessum*, with her cigars and quenchless appetite for local professors. Wagner felt a month of her would be the death of him; nor did they meet again till 1876.

TRISTAN UND MATHILDE

That December Wagner noted down the first musical ideas for the *Tristan* love scene, content with them for the moment as a musical offering to Mathilde. He described Mathilde to Frau Wille as 'one of those absolutely happy women for whom nothing counts but home, husband and child'. At *Tristan* time, in April 1857, when the Brazilian envoy at Dresden had requested on behalf of the Emperor an Italian opera for Rio de Janeiro, and Wagner thought he saw his way to quick completion of a popular and passionate success, the situation was less clear-cut. Otto Wesendonck had bought a large property on the 'Green hill' outside Zürich; he offered the Wagners for a nominal rent the small neighbouring house named by Mathilde 'the Asyl'. The Wagners moved in first, and he described in *Mein Leben* how a Good Friday mood induced thoughts of *Parzival* (it was not actually Good Friday, he later admitted to Cosima). But on his birthday the following month he resumed *Siegfried*, writing at the top of the orchestral sketch '*Tristan* firmly decided'. Inspiration was now split between the two works, and by the end of June he determined to leave young Siegfried beneath the linden tree in Act 2. Some days the urge to finish *The Ring* was nil; but a resurgence of will power took him to the end of the act, the hero in pursuit of the wood-bird, a chase that was to last almost twelve years.

While working on the *Tristan* text, Wagner had as guests at the Asyl Hans von Bülow and his new bride Cosima Liszt, now nineteen. Hans was devoted to her but had written to the father he was 'ready to set her free should she discover

34

she was deceived in me'; Countess d'Agoult, the mother, foresaw no happiness in this marriage for her 'child of passion and liberty'. Minna, Mathilde and Cosima met frequently at the Asyl. They listened with others to readings of the *Tristan* poem, which proved wearying and puzzling to most (Mathilde notably excepted); they reacted severally to extracts from *Siegfried* (Cosima could only weep when asked her opinion). And Bülow luxuriated in 'this glorious, unique man whom one must venerate like a god'. By the end of the year *Tristan* Act 1 was composed, baring new nerves of chromatic harmony, searching emotional depths previously unexplored in music. Mathilde received it with a dedication to 'the angel who had raised him so high'; for her birthday on December 23 there was a performance of *Träume*, a setting of a poem she had written, in Wagner's version for solo violin and small orchestra.

During the winter Mathilde and Wagner immersed themselves in Calderón. Otto felt neglected, Minna slighted, Wagner apprehensive enough to take a break in Paris. There he listened with despair to Berlioz reading the *Trojans* libretto and persuaded Mme Erard to give him a grand piano. Back in Zürich by early February 1858 Wagner found mounting tension on the 'Green hill'. He later told Cosima of Minna's amazement that he could keep silence in the midst of the most terrible scenes, when in fact he was struggling with a *Tristan* idea: 'the two women used to do their best to anger and annoy each other while I was thinking of neither'. The scoring of *Tristan* Act 1 continued, and Otto maintained admirable discretion. But in April, when Minna intercepted a pencil sketch of the *Tristan* prelude on its way to Mathilde wrapped round a letter mainly about Goethe's *Faust*, came the breaking point. Against a background of much-wounded dignity Minna, in poor health because of her heart condition and already dosed with opium, was packed off to a cure at Brestenberg.

Liszt viewed the situation with distaste and described Wagner at the time as resembling 'those high mountains that are radiant at the summit but wrapped in mists up to the shoulder'. Early in May *Tristan* Act 2 was started, and later that month arrived the sixteen-year old Karl Tausig, whirlwind pianist addicted to tea and strong cigars from whom Wagner was careful to keep his schnapps and rum. Other visitors were the tenors Tichatschek and Albert Niemann, one his former Rienzi and Tannhäuser, the other a future Tannhäuser and Siegmund; neither would sing in presence of the other. When Minna, whose death Wagner had been nervously expecting, returned from Brestenberg, a servant welcomed her with a triumphal arch. This was not demolished as soon as courtesy to the neighbours demanded. The Bülows found the Asyl atmosphere 'sultry', and Wagner presided over a 'table surrounded by sad, mysteriously depressed guests'. The Countess d'Agoult brought moments of distinction, carefully, ironically showing Minna how to pile the cushions on her sofa: 'pas un de trop'. The composition of *Tristan* Act 2 was complete; the Bülows departed in tears (Cosima with an unexpected display of emotion threw herself at Wagner's feet); Minna advertised the effects cheaply owing to sudden removal; and Wagner left on August 7.

His destination was Venice. At Lausanne he was joined by Karl Ritter, who also was despatching an abandoned wife to Saxony. Wagner settled himself at the Palazzo Giustiniani on the Grand Canal, where a refurbishing with new hangings was seen by a sympathetic police councillor (Venice was Austrian territory and officially curious about Wagner) as evidence for the composer's poor nerves. Wagner was sensitive to the melancholy of the decaying buildings, watched entranced while 'like a deep dream the fairy city of lagoons lay stretched in shade before me', and listened in the night silence to the lonely cry of gondoliers, which in turn suggested the unfathomable sadness of the *Tristan* shepherd's tune. Despite illness, *Tristan* Act 2 was fully scored on 18 March 1859, and Mathilde's spirit had received a commentary on Wagner's progress and moods in his Venice diary.

He enjoyed the company of Austrian officers, had hospitality at the barracks, heard his music played by military bands. Yet there was threat of extradition from Venice and at the end of March he made for Switzerland again. In Lucerne, at the Schweizerhof hotel, he was cared for by Verena Weidmann, who later worked for him in Munich and Tribschen and had 'never met a man who was so full of gratitude for anything that was done for him'. There was leisurely exercise on an old horse called Lise, visits to the Wesendoncks for appearances' sake, steady work on *Tristan* Act 3. This harrowing act, which in 1882 Wagner thought more than one could endure from the stage, tortured him 'to the last degree' in composition. An alphorn on the heights of the Rigi gave him the shepherd's merry song; the rest of a music that almost terrified him came he knew not whence. The score was completed on August 6.

LITTLE CHANGE IN PARIS

Perhaps *Tristan* was 'too far outside the possibilities of the present' for performance; Wagner hoped nonetheless, and founded his hopes on Paris, made financially possible through Otto Wesendonck, who bought rights in *Rheingold* and *Walküre* for 12,000 francs. Wagner paid in advance for the lease of a house in the Rue Newton, soon to be demolished to the greater glory of Haussmann's Paris; employed a maid and liveried ex-Swiss guard; and awaited Minna's arrival in November with what he could summon of the 'meekness, steadfastness, benevolence and indulgence' urged by Dr Pusinelli of Dresden. Minna curtailed the household, Wagner settled to a scheme for three concerts at the beginning of 1860. For these he wrote a concert ending to the *Tristan* prelude and redemptive conclusion to the *Dutchman* overture.

Bülow helped with the concerts and stayed with Liszt's mother. Wagner issued no press tickets; the first rehearsal seemed to him 'almost as bad as a riot'; and the presence of Auber, Berlioz, Gounod and Meyerbeer helped neither appreciation of his aims nor his finances. Even Berlioz was incredulous of the *Tristan* prelude, into which Wagner had nursed the orchestra almost note by note. The reviews had little expectation for 'the music of the future'. After the third concert Baudelaire wrote to Wagner: 'You, sir, are not the first man in connection with whom I have had to suffer and blush for my countrymen'. And a 10,000 franc deficit was crippling (he had now, with Wesendonck's consent, sold *Rheingold* to Schott for 10,000 francs; the concerts were to have provided the 6,000 to buy off Otto).

Despite hostility and incomprehension, Wagner gathered a sympathetic circle about him in the Rue Newton. His salons and music-makings were attended by the director of the Louvre; by Gustav Doré, who portrayed Wagner conducting an orchestra of spirits among mountains; by Saint-Saëns and Gounod; by Liszt's elder daughter Blandine (Minna found her common if not vulgar and there were stories of indiscretion with Wagner); by Malwida von Meysenbug, more congenial now the English Chartists had convinced her the world was not perfectible; and by the Prussian attaché, Count Hatzfeld. A visit to Rossini proved rewarding beyond expectation: there was discussion of *William Tell*, and the veteran composer was rejoiced to find he had been writing 'music of the future' without knowing it. And in the middle of March, as the result of machination at court directed largely by Princess Metternich, wife of the Austrian ambassador and known as 'le singe à la mode' because of her drinking, smoking, swearing and ugliness, Napoleon III commanded *Tannhäuser* at the Opéra.

Two unsuccessful Brussels concerts compounded Wagner's losses; his only profit was in Antwerp, where he was amused by the lack of 'citadel' he had imagined as background to *Lohengrin*. The debts were relieved by Mme Schwabe, who at her Anglesey home had accompanied Malwida von Meysenbug in lieder and was now hostess to Richard Cobden in Paris, and by Marie Kalergis who was rewarded by a runthrough of *Tristan* Act 2 by Pauline Viardot-Garcia and

Wagner, given the orchestral sketches for the work, and later wrote of it as 'an abstraction, intriguing to study' that would everywhere be rejected by the public.

The imperial command for *Tannhäuser* caused embarrassment in Germany. Wagner was still an exile eleven years after the Dresden uprising, and Baron von Seebach, Saxon envoy in Paris, pleaded his case when on leave. Princess Augusta of Prussia spoke directly to the hitherto implacable King John, and in mid-July Wagner was given access to all German principalities but Saxony. In Germany the next month, he had some words with Princess Augusta, who showed languid displeasure (perhaps because of his Saxon accent, a friend close to both suggested). He visited his brother Albert, admirer of his music if not his character. But the fatherland disappointed: 'If I am 'German', he confided to Liszt, 'it is because I carry my Germany within me'.

The director of the Opéra insisted to Wagner at almost every meeting on the need for a ballet in Act 2 of *Tannhäuser*. Wagner discounted the influence of those craving an after-dinner display of ballerinas and enriched the Venusberg scene at the start of Act 1. He was excited that a Napoleon gave him such lavish opportunities in spite of Meyerbeer and the 'embattled hosts of Jewry'. He seemed in the autumn a favourite at the Opéra, unopposed in his lightest whim. While engaged in *Tannhäuser* revisions he had to move house; a typhoid fever then laid him so low he was blind for a while and deliriously wished to go to Naples for conversations with Garibaldi.

Morale at the Opéra had slipped. Musically *Tannhäuser* was troubled by a recalcitrant Niemann, who played the lead; and by the conductor Dietsch, whom Bülow accused of a 'wretched memory and imbecile fumbling'. But the staging was entrancing and, even if Paris might be baffled by Tannhäuser's dilemma and insufficiently disapprove of Venus's ways, expectations were high. Auber shared the general glee there would be much worth watching. 'Those are indeed voluptuous sounds', Wesendonck had remarked at a Venusberg rehearsal; Wagner wondered whether Otto feared he had danced like that in front of Mathilde.

The three performances in March 1861 were 'a fiasco such as has probably never been known before in Paris', wrote the Tannhäuser. Hooting, hissing, shouting, fighting, the blowing of 'Wagner whistles', quarter-hour interruptions to the stage action, meant the opera was hardly heard. Wagner stayed at home drinking tea during the third performance. Berlioz felt he was 'cruelly avenged'; so too was Meyerbeer when the *Tannhäuser* costumes were diverted to *Robert the devil*. Princess Metternich swore that at least the Viennese aristocracy would not have yelled for an Act 2 ballet in *Fidelio*; but Baron von Seebach said nothing, as he had lost his voice shouting in Wagner's support.

Failure of the Paris *Tannhäuser* made a *Tristan* success the more urgent. First plans centred on Karlsruhe, and Wagner went to Vienna in search of a suitable Tristan and Isolde. Some time before, Wagner had told Berlioz he hoped he would not one day prove the only German who had not yet seen *Lohengrin*. In Vienna he heard it rehearsed and was moved to his foundations. He described the scene to Minna: 'I sat there quite still all the time, while one tear after another ran down my cheek. The dear people came quietly and embraced me. At the close the orchestra and chorus broke into loud cheers!' The intendant now suggested *Tristan* for Vienna.

Back in Paris he received money from Liszt, who was so absorbed in the social whirl that he had time for his daughter Blandine only in a carriage between engagements. Wagner wrote an Album Leaf for Prince Metternich that suggested *Die Meistersinger* (*The Mastersingers*) was already astir; and in July he composed a companion piece for Countess Pourtalès combining a *Tannhäuser* motif with Tristanesque harmonies and called 'Arrival at the black swans' (there was a pair in the garden). The previous month it was the *Lohengrin* white swan that had bewitched the fifteen-year old Prince Ludwig of Bavaria at a performance he had specially requested.

During a reluctant visit to Weimar he heard an impressive *Faust* symphony from Liszt. He went on with Blandine and her husband to a meeting with Cosima, who was taking a milk cure at Reichenhall and gave him a 'look of almost timid questioning as they parted' (Minna considered this other Liszt daughter also 'rather fast'). Disconsolate in September 1861 that *Tristan* chances seemed dogged in Vienna by the tenor Ander and his 'lax vocal chords', Wagner eagerly accepted a Wesendonck invitation to visit the family in Venice. He claimed it was there, in front of Titian's Assumption, that the *Meistersinger* idea revived after lying dormant since 1845.

ROOTLESS MASTERSINGERS

His mind was already fired with music for the *Meistersinger* prelude and the mischievous conceit of naming the marker 'Hanslich' after his detested Vienna critic, Eduard Hanslick. The composer Peter Cornelius, loyal Wagner companion of the time, procured him antique sources from the Royal Library, and Wagner threw himself energetically into the task of recreating mediaeval Nuremberg. He was convinced, as he told the publisher Schott, he would be striking a properly German chord and the subject would yet appeal to foreigners as well.

The Metternichs suggested he should be their guest in Paris, an arrangement that had to be cancelled when the Princess's father lost his wife and part of his reason. Wagner read the *Meistersinger* prose sketch to a gathering at Schott's in Mainz; he then stayed in Paris at the Hotel Voltaire, across the Seine from the Louvre, to work at the poem. He enjoyed bringing to life the angular citizens of old Nuremberg with one eye on the Tuileries and told Mathilde Wesendonck she must fortify herself against the charms of Sachs. The poem was done in thirty days. 'Wach' auf!' was conceived on a walk to the Taverne Anglaise through the arcades of the Palais Royal; and on 31 January 1862 the finished text was read to Countess Pourtalès. There were other readings of the poem, at Schott's (Cornelius came specially through floods and floating ice), then to the Grand Duke and Duchess of Baden in a room where Goethe was depicted declaiming the first scenes of *Faust*.

The previous November had been the twenty-fifth anniversary of a marriage now in disarray. Minna wrote to Emma Herwegh: 'I received as present from my husband a gold bracelet and leave of absence for a whole year'; in return she sent Wagner some leaves from a silver-spangled wreath given by friends. In February 1862 Wagner suggested she should join him at Biebrich on the Main, where he was then settling in. On the 21st she unexpectedly arrived, as did a letter of thanks for the *Mastersingers* poem and a delayed Christmas present from Mathilde. Minna reacted strongly, and Wagner described the episode as ten days of hell. Minna returned to Dresden, and there was no further attempt to live together. In June Wagner tentatively raised with Pusinelli the idea of a judicial separation; Minna was outraged and the subject dropped. Comfort of a kind Wagner found with Friederike Meyer, an intelligent actress in Frankfurt; and in the gentle disposition of Mathilde Maier, later friend of Nietzsche.

By the end of March Wagner had a complete amnesty from Dresden, where he had no intention of returning because of Minna; and an evening view of Mainz crystallised for him much of the *Mastersingers* prelude. Work on the opera was fitful. The prelude to Act 3 was shaped on his birthday before writing to thank Countess Pourtalès for 1200 thalers; the Johannistag address of Pogner (who was Wagner's tribute to Otto Wesendonck) was interrupted when his servant Lise had a fit; Pogner had no sooner introduced Walther to the guild than Wagner was bitten by a bulldog. At the beginning of July the Bülows came to Biebrich. Cosima read to keep Wagner still while having his portrait painted for Wesendonck (to commemorate Mathilde's latest confinement); Bülow's tenderness to him almost made Cosima jealous: 'To have Wagner as a neighbour means that everything else shrivels into insignificance'. Cornelius and Tausig kept clear, smoking a glorious cigar in his honour; and Wagner knew why: 'I was obviously a tyrant to them'. But a new ease with Cosima culminated in an offer, ultimately retracted, to transport her by wheelbarrow across a Frankfurt square.

Mastersingers progress was too slow for Schott, who declined to make further advances: 'A music publisher cannot provide for your requirements; that could only be done by an enormously rich banker or by some prince with millions at his disposal'. Wagner was hurt: 'A good deal can be extorted from a man by hunger, but not works of a lofty kind'. The prelude was first heard at a poorly attended Leipzig concert in November. Cosima was there, pale and in black because of Blandine's death in childbed. Hans seemed cheerful, but members of Wagner's family were upset by Richard's and Cosima's mirth. A brief and final visit to Minna in Dresden was chaperoned by his sister Klara. Wagner then arrived in Vienna with Friederike Meyer, antagonising her sister, his hitherto loyal Isolde. A confused year continued with Wagner's reading the *Mastersingers* to a group including Hanslick, lampooned as the marker and naturally upset; and ended with a new preface to the *Ring* poem taking up Schott's hint and pleading eloquently for court backing: 'Will this prince be found? In the beginning was the deed!'

There was no sign of the prince in 1863, which began with concerts in Vienna, Prague and Russia. For Vienna the 'unassuming and good-natured' Brahms helped with copying of extracts from *Meistersinger* and *The Ring*; deficits were crowned by a recklessly extravagant dinner with repeated calls for champagne. In Prague Dvořák was among the violas and there was some profit. The way to St Petersburg was *via* the Bülows in Berlin. Cosima was pregnant with her second child, to be called Blandine. The Russian visit had been prepared by Marie Kalergis and associated Wagner with the critic Serov and composer Anton Rubinstein. There were successful concerts in St Petersburg and Moscow. The Muscovites gave him a snuff-box inscribed 'Doch einer kam' (a reference to the arrival of spring in *Die Walküre* Act 1);

43

the imprisoned debtors of St Petersburg, for whom he conducted a charity concert, responded with a silver drinking-horn; and at four tea parties he read *The Ring* to the Grand Duchess Helena and her ladies in waiting.

With seven thousand thalers from Russia, Wagner settled comfortably in Penzing, a Viennese suburb. The rooms were draped and hung, servants employed, and the cellar was stocked. He summoned Mathilde Maier and was 'grievously shocked' when she declined. Friederike Meyer wrote that she would like to see him again; for the moment, though he later agreed with Cosima that Friederike was the most interesting of his female friends, he decided to keep her in reserve (in fact they met no more). To commemorate his fiftieth birthday, during which he felt very isolated, Viennese students and choral societies organised a torchlight procession in June, the month *Meistersinger* scene 1 was fully scored.

Further concerts took Wagner to Budapest, in November to Prague and Karlsruhe, where a two hundred mark profit was spent on a two hundred and twenty mark fur coat (he managed to get twenty marks knocked off), and where Turgeniev admired the 'Ride of the Valkyries' but loathed 'Wotan's farewell', performed, as Wagner admitted, by a 'voiceless but well-drilled vaudeville singer'. A last stay at the Wesendoncks' left Wagner incredulous: 'the idea of assisting me did not seem even to dawn on these friends of mine'. After a night with Mathilde Maier's family he was in Berlin on November 28. He sold a snuff-box from the Duke of Baden and took a carriage drive with Cosima during which 'with tears and sobs we sealed our confession to belong to each other alone' (this became one of Cosima's holy days). That evening they saw Gluck's *Paris and Helen*. In Breslau he went to a concert attended only by Jews in the company of Eliza Wille's sister Frau von Bissing. She promised money but then with some passion withdrew the offer: 'Well then, in God's name, *No!*', on the ground that whatever she did for him he would love only the Wesendonck woman.

Back in Vienna for Christmas, he gave each of his friends

'an appropriate trifle'. Cornelius described his: 'The mad Wagner has fixed up a big Christmas tree, and underneath it a royally rich table for me. Just imagine a marvellous heavy overcoat, and elegant grey dressing gown, a red scarf, a blue cigar-case'; and the list continues to encompass what 'only an oriental imagination could think of'. Wagner could now keep going only through money-lenders at crippling rates of interest. He read the *Iliad* with Cornelius (skipping the catalogue of ships); hopes of another Russian tour were dashed by a Polish uprising; and at the beginning of March the Vienna *Tristan* was finally abandoned as unperformable. Thoughts of death oppressed him and he started bequeathing books and manuscripts. With little to keep him in Vienna and much to drive him out, Wagner fled on March 23 rather than face his creditors.

On Good Friday he was in Munich. He saw the portrait of the eighteen-year old Ludwig II who had ascended the throne a fortnight before; and he wrote a bitter verse epitaph on his life's failure. Temporary refuge was offered at Mariafeld. François Wille was in Constantinople, Eliza ready with hospitality while Wagner sat 'huddled in his Karlsruhe fur coat'; read Frederick the Great's diaries, George Sand, Walter Scott; dreamed he was King Lear on the heath and had joined Voltaire at the Prussian court. After a month he left with Eliza 'a last letter, a holy letter' for Mathilde, wandered aimlessly to Stuttgart and saw *Don Giovanni*. A member of the cast, the Jewish baritone and later impresario Angelo Neumann, heard him pacing the hotel room in squeaky boots like a caged lion. 'I am at the end of the road', he wrote to a friend; late on the second day a visiting card in French from Franz Seraph von Pfistermeister, cabinet secretary of the Bavarian king, was handed him; and on the third day Wagner's life was transformed by the gift of a photograph from Ludwig, a ring, and a message that the king's ardour to see the poet and composer of *Lohengrin* matched the glow of its precious stone.

That day, May 3, Wagner wrote to Ludwig: 'Now the

marvels of poetry have come as a divine reality into my poor, loveless life'; the king replied: 'I will repay you everything to the best of my ability'. As a boy Ludwig had sealed letters with a cross and swan; for Christmas 1858 his tutor had given him *Opera and drama*; he had read the *Ring* poem on the lake at Hohenschwangau, studied the prose works, commanded *Lohengrin* a second time in February 1864. 'My mission', Ludwig wrote later to Cosima, 'is to live for him, to suffer for him if that is necessary for his salvation'. And Wagner to Bülow was similarly exalted: 'I myself have begotten it for myself out of the depths of my longing and my suffering. Only to me could anything of the kind have happened . . . and a queen had to bear this son for me'.

CROWN AND THORNS

The immediate practicalities of the matter were to settle Wagner's debts and establish him on Lake Starnberg near the king. Wagner's bliss was soon modified by loneliness; on June 30 he wrote to Eliza Wille: 'it is only on the highest mountain peaks, as it were, that I can maintain myself with this young king'. And in fact Cosima von Bülow had arrived the previous day with her two children, after Wagner had already sent distress signals to Heinrich Porges, a Jewish disciple, to Cornelius, and to Mathilde Maier (she might come as a quasi-niece, he suggested). Cosima and Richard were faithful to their vow of the previous November and Wagner in his happiness sketched themes he thought might do for quartets but which eventually found their home in *Siegfried* Act 3 and the *Siegfried Idyll*. Bülow came later and spent a vile summer, ill to the point of paralysis and nervously wrecked. Liszt visited briefly and wondered at the humour and vivacity of *Die Meistersinger*, 'lively and beautiful, like Shakespeare'; Wagner penned the *Huldigungsmarsch*, homage to the king who now made so much possible.

On September 26 Wagner affirmed to the king his determination to press ahead with *The Ring*. The following day he worked on the full score of *Siegfried* Act 1 and was offered a spacious home at 21 Briennerstrasse, the furnishings of which were mocked a few months later in the Munich *Punch*: 'A magnificent bedroom: velvet hangings, silk curtains, wool carpets, mirrored ceilings with frescoes by Pecht and Kaulbach. Towards the window a small orange grove, in which from time to time a ripe fruit falls to the ground'. The first performance of the *Huldigungsmarsch* in October seemed sad, he and Cosima remembered in 1878; it was dull and cold in the Residence garden, the king stood at his window, and there was no one else around. 'All humbug', Pfistermeister noted in his diary. Ludwig now became the third owner of *The Ring* (after Wesendonck and Schott), for which there were plans to build a special theatre designed by Gottfried Semper, architect of the Dresden opera house, and to found a music school in Munich.

By the end of 1864 the Bülows had received a royal summons to Munich, Wagner opera performances had been launched with a *Flying Dutchman*, and Baron von der Pfordten, education minister in Saxony at the time of the revolution, became head of the Bavarian king's ministry. Early in 1865 there were signs the Munich balance might be disturbed. Wagner was visited by a Frau Dangl who asked him whether he believed in the stars and told him the king's future was largely in his hands. 'The fate of this wonderful, unique youth is entrusted to me, *me*', he wrote to Mathilde Maier. Wagner's influence was such it was worth cultivating and he claimed later he had been offered two theatres, two music schools by rival Jesuit and court factions. To Pfistermeister he one day called the king 'Mein junge'; royal coolness followed and Wagner was denied access to the presence. Towards the end of February the press made a first attempt to drive a wedge between king and favourite. Wagner wondered whether he should leave Munich; Ludwig bade him stay: 'everything will be as glorious as before'. Cornelius observed that the friendliest letters passed between them but they hardly met.

Tristan, classified by the state librarian under 'musica

theoretica', was to be produced that summer. On April 10 Bülow conducted the first orchestral rehearsal and Cosima's third daughter Isolde was born. Parentage was not in dispute and Cosima testified as much when there was a court case next century; for the present Wagner acted as godfather. Bülow caused scandal in the city by referring to potential *Tristan* patrons as 'Schweinehunde', but for the open rehearsal on May 11 Ludwig pardoned all those who had taken part in the 1849 revolution. Four days later Wagner's Paris debt to Mme Schwabe of Anglesey threatened unpleasantness which the privy purse averted; Pusinelli wrote that Minna was dying (a false alarm); and Malvina Schnorr, the Isolde, was taken ill. Postponement meant the Munich Volkstheater got in first with a parody 'opera of the future', *Tristanderl und Süssholde*. But of the four *Tristan* performances beginning on June 10 Bülow wrote: 'It is the greatest success that a new Wagner work has ever had anywhere. The Schnorrs were incredible' in the name parts. It was fifteen years since *Lohengrin* had been produced in Weimar. Liszt had now taken minor orders in Rome and didn't come to *Tristan*. Ludwig was effusive: 'Entirely for you, ardently loved one, did I come into the world'. Pfistermeister was exasperated: '*This accursed Tristan!* The devil make off with the musicians'.

Wagner had watched Ludwig Schnorr's Tristan with deep emotion, correcting little at rehearsal but silently embracing the dying hero. Schnorr left Munich in mid-July after taking part in a private concert for the king. On July 21, the day Wagner began dictating to Cosima 'that true book of righteousness' as she called the autobiographical *Mein Leben*, he heard Schnorr was dead, with the parting words: 'Farewell Siegfried. Console my Richard'. Wagner and Bülow made for the funeral in Dresden but arrived too late. 'My king, in this singer I have lost much', he wrote to Ludwig. After a stay with the king in Schloss Berg, Wagner spent the middle of August in a royal hunting lodge, where at the outset he had to wander for water in a white dressing gown by the light of the moon. The weather was villainous, he read Hugo's *Les misérables* and, inspired by the Indian *Ramayana*, thought of himself and Cosima 'united in a better climate by the Ganges'. Here he began jottings in the Brown Book, while his servant Franz had the job of keeping off tourists. Back in Munich, at the end of the month he wrote the first prose sketch of *Parzival* (its then name) in response to the king's request.

'I am the most German of men, I am the German spirit', Wagner confided to the Brown Book. In mid-September he wrote for Ludwig *What is German?*, praising the people which had discovered Shakespeare, indicating as 'German' the pursuit of the beautiful without thought of profit, fame or recognition. 'I must not consider myself sole lessee of the German spirit', he was told by a north German paper. Munich dislike for Wagner, nicknamed Lolus or Lolotte after a previous king's mistress Lola Montez, and for Cosima the 'carrier pigeon' grew during the autumn of 1865. An October request for forty thousand gulden was paid to Cosima by treasury officials partly in sacks of coin; the Munich *Punch* had already pointed out that while the old Orpheus animated the rocks, the new one made money bags dance, to an infinite melody. And the Brown Book noted 'The king's love is a crown of thorns'. In November the towers of Hohenschwangau re-echoed to *Lohengrin* fanfares, Wagner read extracts there from *Mein Leben* to Ludwig's attentive amusement, and Prince Paul von Taxis, the king's aide, came across the lake in a swan-boat illuminated by electricity. But by the end of the month a crisis had developed through a Wagner newspaper article suggesting 'the removal of two or three persons' from the king's entourage. Von der Pfordten told the king on December 1 he must choose between Wagner and his loyal subjects. 'My dear minister', he replied, 'my resolution stands firm. R Wagner must leave Bavaria'. This he did on December 10.

THE SWISS FAMILY WAGNER

An entry in the Brown Book of 22 January 1866, 'Cut, cut, my sword, that the heart of a king may learn what real suffering is' was superfluous. With Wagner wandering between Switzerland and France, Ludwig was close to abdication and suicide, kneeling in prayer and tears before Wagner's bust. At Marseilles Wagner heard from Pusinelli that Minna had died on the morning of January 25; he did not attend the funeral, for which buglers of the royal orchestra played and a local choral society sang. Back in Geneva he devised a ritual for his dead dog Pohl. Loathing for Munich mingled in his mind with affection for Nuremberg as he headed for completion of *Meistersinger* Act 1 on March 23; in Nuremberg might be the future seat of government, there might arise his new music school. And the king might give him a castle lodge at Bayreuth.

Cosima and her eldest daughter Daniela came to Geneva on March 8; dictation of *Mein Leben* was resumed the next day; and by the end of the month they had seen Tribschen, Wagner's home on a promontary near Lucerne for the next six years which for private etymological reasons he spelt 'Triebschen'. Soon after moving in, Wagner wrote gleefully to Bülow: 'Johannistag! Johannistag! Hans Sachs–Hans Bülow!', suggesting the two households should merge in Switzerland. Cosima and the three children arrived on May 12, Bülow the following month. Wagner now began *Meistersinger* Act 2, and for his birthday on the 22nd the king, persuaded by Wagner to consider state business rather than abdication, arrived at Tribschen and was announced as Walther von Stolzing.

Munich was aghast the king should visit the 'debtmaker' at a time of political crisis, leaving Bavaria when war between Prussia and Austria was imminent. He was given a chill reception when he opened parliament at the end of May. Still needing Bülow as conductor in Munich, Wagner now made a bold bid to clear the trio's reputation. Cosima wrote to the king: 'My royal lord, I have three children, to

50

whom it is my duty to transmit their father's honourable name unstained'; and Ludwig was persuaded to sign a Wagner letter to the papers upholding the morality of the situation. The letter was published on June 14 the day Bavaria joined Austria against Prussia; it enhanced nobody's reputation. Two days later Prince Hohenlohe wrote in his diary: 'The king sees no one now. He is staying with Taxis on the Rose Island and lets off fireworks'. Bavaria was defeated at Kissingen on July 10.

Meistersinger made good progress throughout the summer, the Act 2 orchestral sketch complete in September, Act 3 composition started at the beginning of October. The young Hans Richter moved in as secretary and copyist, overwhelmed at proximity to such creative power, 'happy in the consciousness of being really liked by the greatest man of all time'. But the autumn was clouded from an unexpected direction. Wagner wrote to his friend Röckel that he was in for another hair-raising adventure: 'Frau Schnorr is on the point of going out of her mind'. It was not quite that, but she was much influenced since her husband's death by Isidore von Reutter, a medium with 'the figure of a military policeman' convinced she should marry the king and Frau Schnorr should marry Wagner, while he ought to 'make smaller demands on the human voice and write songs'. Cosima was the stumbling block, so Malvina wrote to the king that the Tribschen relationship was adulterous. Cornelius saw it in terms of the *Magic Flute*: the Starry queen had now written far too strongly to Tamino; Sarastro-Wagner had after all constructed a temple for the whole cast. Frau Schnorr was barred Munich, but Ludwig's eyes were opened.

At the beginning of 1867 Wagner noted in his annals 'Parzival engaged'. The king had indeed contracted to marry his cousin Sophie, and it was hoped the *Mastersingers* would be ready to crown the wedding day. Meanwhile a June *Lohengrin* was cause of friction: Wagner had engaged the ageing Tichatschek from Dresden for the name part; Ludwig's every instinct was affronted when this 'knight of

51

the rueful countenance' appeared in the swan-boat. Ludwig insisted on a new Lohengrin. Wagner left Munich instantly, and though there came later, as reported in the annals, a 'repentant letter from the king' in which he appeared to grovel to the extent of kissing 'the hand which struck' him, Ludwig had found his strength and a new appreciation of Wagner's character. Neither of them attended an August *Tannhäuser* under Bülow: there was court mourning for Otto of Greece in Munich, sulking and *Meistersinger* at Tribschen.

German art and German politics, a Wagnerian treatise serialised during the autumn of 1867, put the responsibility for Germany's deepest woe on Leibnitz, who recognised Louis XIV as destined ruler of the world. There was discussion of the 'youthful German breast, still heaving with noble aspiration', and indignation that Mme Rigolboche, the Parisian cancan dancer, should be summoned to a German theatre. Liszt, disturbed by the Cosima situation, visited Wagner during October, a 'Napoleon at St Helena'. 'Dreaded but enjoyable', was Wagner's comment in the annals. Liszt was moved by Wagner's loneliness, but for comfort could only point at a portrait of the king. *Meistersinger* was brought out; 'no one but he could have produced such a masterpiece', thought Liszt; Bülow considered it 'the culmination of his genius'. It was completed at 8 p.m. on October 24, less than a fortnight after Ludwig broke off his engagement. The anti-French tone of Wagner's articles reached such a point in December, with talk of a new power emerging in history 'before which French power will pale for ever', that the king forbade further publication.

Wagner at Tribschen was depressed, Ludwig hurt and exasperated; the result was a long silence. In March 1868 this was broken by Ludwig, 'alone in the loveless, empty, desolate world', unable to endure lack of Wagnerian news. In Munich later that month, Wagner commented in the annals: 'My arrival appears to delight the king. He allows himself neither to be heard nor seen'. Activities that spring included sketches for a *Romeo and Juliet* funeral symphony; a deeply felt and generous article on the first Tristan, Ludwig Schnorr; further work on the Buddhist project, *The Victors*; and plans for a complete edition of his prose works, given a first tentative ordering in the Brown Book.

Ludwig made a birthday journey with him on the steamer Tristan to the Rose Island in Lake Starnberg. There was now a month in Munich for *Meistersinger* rehearsals, at which Wagner exercised all the charm, energy and patience he could always command with musicians. The first performance was planned for midsummer day (Bruckner had been allowed to give the final scene in April) and, though Saint-Saëns saw Hans Sachs's closing address as 'the cry of pan-Germanism and war on the Latin races', and there were those who felt Wagner's character had deteriorated over the last three years, the occasion was felicitous and successful. Bülow conducted; Jessie Laussot, Mathilde Maier and Malwida von Meysenbug were there; Liszt was in Rome hearing Mass in the Sistine Chapel, playing to the Pope and receiving cigars. There was offence that Wagner should acknowledge applause from the royal box, whither Ludwig had summoned him during the prelude. Cosima wished they could have enjoyed the work together, noting later in her diary that when future generations refreshed themselves with its unique qualities, they should remember 'beneath what tears those smiles had flowered'.

Ludwig's pleasure was heroically expressed: 'To you I owe everything, everything! Hail German art! In this sign will we conquer!'; Wagner's almost submissively: 'You are the rescuer, the redeemer! See me here speechless at your feet!' They had now met for the last time till the *Ring* performances of 1876. Two other friendships lapsed that summer. Laube, early helper and publisher of the *Autobiographical sketch*, wrote unfavourably of *Meistersinger* and was dismissed with scurrilous verses; Röckel joined the anti-Cosima camp and made damaging revelations to the king. Cornelius came to Tribschen and continued his detached

53

observations: 'When you see an aviary with golden pheasants and other rare birds, you can't help saying to yourself, God bless us, what must all this be costing the man'. Wagner made sketches of a play to be called *Luther's marriage* and of the little comedy based on his Magdeburg experience.

'The adventurous journey of Herr Will and Frau Vorstel' was how Wagner and Cosima referred to their Italian trip of autumn 1868. Schopenhauer's *Die Welt als Will und Vorstellung* provided the names, which they used also in telegrams. Appalling weather dogged them as they made a way through raging torrents; but the experience was decisive. Early in October Cosima wrote to Bülow, later in the month Wagner to Ludwig: 'Illusion could no longer prevail! . . . There is nothing for me to do but stand by her: may you, kind and noble one, range yourself faithfully by my side in this matter!' Ludwig did not reply till the following February; nor did he receive Wagner in November when on his way to Leipzig. There Wagner met the young Nietzsche, overflowing with *Tristan* and vastly entertained to hear extracts from *Mein Leben* on Wagner's student days. On November 16 Cosima arrived at Tribschen with Isolde, Eva (born on 17 February 1867), and her loyalties clear.

Tribschen was 'the nunnery of my choice which has redeemed me from the world and purified me'. Her love for Wagner was a new birth; her cross was absence of the elder daughters and consuming guilt towards Hans. Liszt, too had written: 'Passion passes, remorse remains'. Dictation of *Mein Leben* was taken up on the third day, by the end of the year *Siegfried* Act 1 was scored, and Wagner was writing a new preface to *Jewishness in music*. He quickly settled down to a happy and productive work routine. After a morning at his desk and lunch, he went for a walk with the dogs as described to Ludwig in February 1869: 'At three I put on my large and intimidating Wotan hat and embark on my regular walk accompanied by Russ and Kos—Falstaff with his pages!'

For Ludwig 1869 was a building year, with a start on

remodelling Linderhof after the manner of Louis XIV and plans for the mediaeval splendours of Neuschwanstein. Wagner began with the reissue of *Jewishness*, which caused Cosima qualms and made Bülow gasp, 'Lord of heaven, what a shindy there'll be'. Using Mathilde Wesendonck's gold pen, Cosima started her diary and they read the *Odyssey* together. In February Ludwig at last wrote, announcing a *Rheingold* for the summer after a June *Tristan*. Tribschen reaction was gloomy. But Wagner's concerns were mainly creative and domestic: 'What a happy old ass I am!'; while Cosima tried to prevent an explosion when the little Isolde didn't like the latest bit of *Siegfried*. In March Berlioz died, 'the giant pupil too great to find a master'; and in May Nietzsche, now at twenty-five Basel professor of classical philology, paid his first Tribschen call, and Wagner was elected to the Royal Academy in Berlin. As he wrote to Malwida von Meysenbug: 'We are happy as lambs; if only there weren't wolves outside'.

After his inaugural on Homer and classical philology, Nietzsche was at Tribschen when Siegfried, Cosima's last child and Wagner's only son, was born. Wagner had grudgingly gratified Cosima's sense of propriety by moving his bed downstairs before the nurse arrived. He took over the diary to describe the birth on June 6 and nature's response with a radiant accompanying sunrise over the mountains. On June 15 Cosima asked Bülow for divorce; he agreed, and congratulated her on the birth he had noticed in the papers. With *Tristan* in June Bülow's misery came full cycle; he resigned from Munich, leaving for Florence and conversations with Jessie Laussot. Despite Wagner's wishes, *Rheingold* was to follow under Richter, who came to study the score at Tribschen while Cosima embroidered. During July the French delegation led by the 'hurricane' Judith Mendès-Gautier blew in. Judith noticed the intense blue of Wagner's eyes as he gazed over the lake; was entranced as he climbed trees and scaled the house; treated the work-desk with almost exaggerated reverence. His step-sister

55

Cäcilie and her husband came and were thought 'not very pleasant'. And the Serovs from Russia, he claiming Wagner's name had been carved near a waterfall in Finland, she 'hateful as night and interested in the liberation of women'.

Wagner had unbounded faith in destiny since his son's birth and was working high-spiritedly on the orchestral sketch of *Siegfried* Act 3. The 'buffo duet' between Wotan and Siegfried had gone well and destiny's only unpleasantness was the Munich *Rheingold*. At the open rehearsal on August 27 attended by the king (Liszt was there too), a Rhinemaiden was sick in her swimming contraption, and it was clear there were problems. Next day Richter sent Wagner a telegram: 'Orchestra very good; Liszt and others have expressed their satisfaction. Prevent performance at any cost!' The reason for drastic action was deficiencies in the staging. Wagner encouraged Richter and the Wotan to resign. It was now a battle of wills between Ludwig and Wagner. At the end of the month the king telegraphed his court secretary: 'Vivat Düfflipp; pereat theatre rabble!'; and then 'If Wagner dares to offer any more opposition, his allowance is to be taken from him for ever'. Wagner made an abortive visit to Munich. Ludwig fumed: 'J'en ai assez'; found another conductor, to whom Wagner wrote roughly 'Hands off my score!'; and *Rheingold* was performed on September 22.

One day Cosima noted Wagner had fallen asleep after weeping bitterly over the king's behaviour. Could he honourably continue to draw his royal pension? In October he took up the *Götterdämmerung* Norns' scene with its 'rustles of the night' he had sketched nineteen years before. That same month Ludwig apologised for his actions and there was a newspaper announcement that *Walküre* was to be done in Munich the following year. For Christmas 1869 Nietzsche was at Tribschen and Cosima read the *Parzival* sketch with him. Wagner had received from Cäcilie copies of letters his step-father had written his mother, and from Cosima a reprint of Geyer's play *The slaughter of the innocents*. Wagner convinced himself Geyer was his true father; Nietzsche had been given proofs of *Mein Leben* to see through the press and the commission for the 'vulture' crest that should proclaim Wagner's present view of his parentage.

At the start of 1870 the proofs were tried out on Otto Wesendonck who gave displeasure by recommending less intimate detail in future. In February *Die Meistersinger* was performed for the first time at the Vienna opera. The Jews were under the misconception that Beckmesser's serenade was a parody of a synagogue chant; hence a major disturbance making Angelo Neumann as the nightwatchman inaudible at the end of Act 2. On March 5 Wagner happened to mention Bayreuth: the discovery in an encyclopaedia that its Bibiena theatre had the largest stage in Germany seemed significant. That day was henceforth 'the birthday of Bayreuth'.

Cosima suffered much from the ecstatic tone of the king's letters, Wagner more from their content. Concerning *Walküre* Ludwig wrote: 'It is for you that I wear my crown: tell me what your will is and I will obey. But do not deprive me of the very atmosphere of my existence by forbidding me the production of your works'. Wagner besought him to have *Walküre* done privately; it was publicly performed on June 26. Liszt was there and went on to Oberammergau; Cosima was kept busy cutting out and destroying unfavourable reviews. An expedition to Pilatus, the peak overlooking Tribschen, was prelude to the divorce from Bülow on July 18 and the French declaration of war against Prussia the following day. In spite of exasperation with Ludwig and talk of transferring to a Paris garret, Richard and Cosima were married in the local protestant church on August 25, the king's birthday. The witnesses were Malwida von Meysenbug and Hans Richter. Mathilde Wesendonck sent edelweiss, Ludwig a telegram; Liszt admitted to Eliza Wille 'Now my daughter has the man who is worthy of her', but kept addressing her allowance to Baroness von Bülow. Some years later Wagner was elected a member of the 'Amis du divorce'.

1870 was the Beethoven centenary, and the war against France seemed a splendid Beethoven festival, celebrated by

Wagner with an essay linking Beethoven's achievement and Schopenhauer's thought. Napoleon III capitulated on September 2; the following day Fidi (Siegfried) was christened, as fatal to the Napoleons as his father. At Tribschen they read the *Persae* of Aeschylus but thought the misery of France deserved no tragedy, indeed hardly a lament. They went on to the *Peace* of Aristophanes, which Cosima imagined Richard was skipping so as to avoid the grosser indecencies. And during November Wagner too sketched a comedy in the antique manner, *A capitulation*, to be set by Richter to music in the style of Offenbach. His *jeu d'esprit*, mocking equally French culture in the guise of Victor Hugo and the sewer rats of Paris (soon transformed into ballerinas), and German theatre intendants who attempt a cancan with the rats, caused mortal offence to French friends. Countess d'Agoult decided not to visit them for the moment, as they were altogether too German for her. Cosima's birthday was celebrated that year with the *Siegfried Idyll*, into which Wagner wove their most cherished memories.

Though his sister Luise had lost a son-in-law and grandson in the war, Wagner began 1871 in imperial mood. He wrote a poem to the German army encamped before Paris and hoped the French capital, 'the kept woman of Europe', would be destroyed. The crowning of Wilhelm I as German emperor at Versailles inspired the *Kaisermarsch*, which the Wagners learnt later the empress didn't like. An invitation to write a cantata for the London Great Exhibition suggested to Wagner he might submit the *Kaisermarsch* with *God save the Queen* instead of the final 'Volksgesang'. On February 5 he completed the *Siegfried* full score, with Cosima watching over the last notes. As relaxation the Wagners visited the Wesendoncks. Mathilde was now a brunette, and the black hair erased all former memories. From Ludwig Wagner concealed the completion of *Siegfried*, though by the autumn the work was being rehearsed in Munich and plans for the scenery had been made; instead he spoke evasively about schemes for Bayreuth.

In April the Wagners went to Bayreuth. It was immediately clear the baroque splendour of the Bibiena theatre was unsuitable for *The Ring* and they would have to build. In Berlin Cosima was afraid Richard might be murdered by a Jew; but they stayed a fortnight, planning Bayreuth finances with Countess Schleinitz, wife of the minister of the royal household, and with Karl Tausig, who referred to them as 'forces of nature'. Wagner gave a paper on the destiny of opera to the Berlin Academy and also met Bismarck. Wagner found the chancellor 'a great, simple nature'; Bismarck thought Wagner a mountain of conceit.

An 1873 Bayreuth festival was announced from Leipzig on May 12, after the Wagners had heard an Egyptological lecture by Professor Ebers, a Jew and superficial. There was a setback when Tausig died from typhus in July. Wagner wrote a fine epitaph for him, the second of his Jewish help-meets to die (Lehrs was the first). By the end of the year he was encouraged at 'the decision of both municipal councils of Bayreuth to place freely at my disposal the necessary approaches and surround to the site in the neighbourhood of St George's church, chosen for the erection of a festival theatre'. Bayreuth co-operation was exemplary and, though the site was changed twice, local goodwill greatly sustained Wagner. In February 1872 Wagner bought for twelve thousand gulden (a gift from the king) the plot for Wahnfried. Before leaving Tribschen Wagner acquired another Jewish helper in the young Joseph Rubinstein, pianist and member of the 'Nibelung chancellery'. 'I am a Jew', he began his first letter, and wished for redemption through *The Ring*. Nietzsche, who had given immense delight at the beginning of 1872 with his book *The birth of tragedy out of the spirit of music*, spent his twenty-third visit to Tribschen wandering round the emptying rooms at the end of April.

BUILDING BAYREUTH
On 29 April 1872 the first sod was turned at the theatre site. It was Cosima's idea the laying of the foundation stone

on Wagner's 59th birthday should be combined with a performance of the Ninth Symphony. Singers and players came from all over, though Karlsruhe could not cooperate because it was preparing Gounod's *Faust*, and at Dresden Count Platen granted no one leave of absence (an old trumpeter from Wagner's days had wept with vexation). The mayor of Schweinfurth offered to play the timpani and was rejected, while the Schwerin contingent thought it was coming to *The Ring*. On May 22 there was 'rain, rain, not a glimpse of the sun to be seen'. The king telegraphed 'warmest and sincerest congratulations on this day that is so significant for all Germany'; Nietzsche observed Wagner more thoughtful and silent than usual; Liszt was invited but did not attend. Wagner's speech and the symphony gave the impression great things were afoot, and Count Crockow presented Wagner with a leopard shot in Africa.

In June Dr Puschmann of Munich wrote a psychological study proving Wagner insane; on July 22 the orchestral sketch of *Götterdämmerung* Act 3 was completed and Cosima noted his comment: 'Now I have composed the whole poem through; right up to the last word I have been as moved as at the first word'. In August the Countess d'Agoult sent the first volume of her history of the Netherlands, and Cosima was terrified by the first symptoms of Richard's heart trouble. A visit to Liszt in Weimar after some years' coolness was returned in October, when Wagner was sharply jealous of the time Cosima spent with her father. Liszt observed that Cosima was devoted to Wagner like Senta to the Dutchman, and departed to celebrate his birthday in a place secret even from Princess Wittgenstein, who now regarded the Wagners as the moral murderers of Bülow.

At the end of October Cosima was received into the protestant church and Richard took communion with her from Dean Dittmar, a firm friend and counsellor who felt inter-marriage was the solution of the Jewish problem whereas Richard considered Jewish blood too corrosive for blonde blood to resist. A tour of German opera houses in search of

60

Ring singers took much of the time till Christmas. Wagner's account appeared as *The German operatic stage of today*, in which he castigated a Karlsruhe Elisabeth who prayed only to the prompter's box, a Cologne Queen of Night who sang in broad daylight, a Frankfurt *Prophète* so cut as to leave only a few notable extracts, and a mangled *Dutchman* at Mannheim inspiring regret solely for what had not been cut. But there had been a fine *Orfeo* at Dessau, and they had found a future Erda, Waltraute, Gunther and Gurnemanz.

In a protestant mood Wagner would wonder whether to learn the organ and settle down as a Bayreuth cantor; but now he must continue his 'Seven years' war' on behalf of the Nibelungs. *The Ring* was read in Berlin to a gathering including the Egyptologist Lepsius, the scientist Helmholtz, and General Moltke conqueror of the French. At a concert before the imperial pair Wagner concluded with the *Kaisermarsch*; Wilhelm I had slipped away, fearing the choral ending and not wishing to sit through his own praise. In moments of nervous exhaustion after concerts Wagner felt it would be more honourable to tour with lectures on 'What is German?', or just beg for Bayreuth from town to town. His sixtieth birthday was celebrated in the Bibiena theatre with the *New year cantata* of 1835 (Cornelius provided fresh words), his C major overture which be began by attributing to Beethoven or Bellini, and Geyer's *Slaughter of the innocents*.

The Wagners went to Weimar for the successful première of Liszt's *Christus*, and Liszt was in Bayreuth on 2 August 1873 for the topping-out ceremony at the theatre. The building had now reached its highest point, and to Cosima the gigantic framework seemed like an entrance to the underworld, like the foundations of an Egyptian temple, symbolic more of the past than future. When the crown prince visited Bayreuth in September, it was debated whether the unfinished theatre should be lit up. Eventually, Cosima noted, 'like a ghostly apparition, like Wotan's castle it towers up twice in red light'; 'made red by our blood', said Richard.

Bruckner, confused by hero-worship and some beer, could

61

not remember in Bayreuth which of his symphonies Wagner had accepted for dedication; it was no.3. A third of the festival money was in by February 1873, but progress was slow in spite of the Wagner societies initiated by Heckel of Mannheim. It was not very German that the Sultan of Turkey, throttled on the eve of the festival, had taken ten patrons' vouchers and the Khedive of Egypt eleven. A military band in Hamburg sent sixty thalers for the fund, and Bülow was tireless with piano recitals. Wagner took to singing 'quem patronum?' from the Requiem text, then broke Mathilde Wesendonck's gold pen sending out a circular to the patrons. And Ludwig was too busy building to help. By way of encouragement Wagner received the Maximilian order from the king; but Brahms got it at the same time. For Cosima's 1873 birthday he wrote the little *Kinderkatechismus* with piano accompaniment; the children encircled the Christmas tree, while he played waltzes from *Meistersinger*, Strauss and Lanner.

Bayreuth looked bleak at the start of 1874. Wagner thought of approaching the Kaiser direct and making the festival a five-year commemoration of the peace with France. He suggested six overtures to Schott, with such titles as *Lohengrin's sea journey*, *Tristan as hero*, *The dirge for Romeo and Juliet*, *Brünnhilde*, *Wieland the Smith*. Schott paid the ten thousand gulden; Wagner never wrote the music. But on January 25 Ludwig changed his mind: 'No! No and again no! It cannot end thus; help must be given! Our plan cannot come to grief!' Within the month there was agreement for a credit of a hundred thousand thalers, the debt to be repaid from festival profits. The family took over Wahnfried at the end of April, the place where Wagner found 'peace from illusions', named, he said, after a village in Hesse. The locals stared at the sgraffito over the door and the inscription; Cosima wished the front had been left plain but kept quiet.

There were some preliminary *Ring* rehearsals at Wahnfried that summer. Wagner was indefatigable in his care for the music and its interpretation but sometimes discouraged.

62

There was a Rhinemaiden with beautiful voice but no diction; a Mime with not a single consonant; the Woodbird and Erda were intelligent but would vocally have to start from scratch; Amalie Materna as potential Brünnhilde looked beautiful enough from a photo but was dishearteningly plump. Nietzsche, victim already of appalling headaches, was brought to Wahnfried from a hotel where he had been lying ill. He was now growing away from Wagner, gave offence by preferring Latin to German, and caused something of a crisis by continually leaving on the piano Brahms's *Triumphlied*, which he had heard and admired in June. Peter Cornelius, always a little ironical in his admiration, died in October. On November 21 Wagner put the finishing touches to the *Götterdämmerung* full score. What should have been a day of triumph in the family turned to fiery anger on Wagner's side, bewildered suffering on Cosima's. Instead of looking at the desk to see the completed score, Cosima announced a letter from Liszt. The diary noted: 'I had no right to celebrate in joy; I have atoned for the completion with my pain'; she had not the strength to resume entries till December 3.

At Christmas Wagner atoned with a small orchestra accompaniment to the *Kinderkatechismus* and conclusion quoting the final bars of *Götterdämmerung*. From February 1875 there was another concert tour in aid of Bayreuth rehearsals and equipment; Cosima felt they should include Bayreuth hotels, as she was terrified about festival accommodation. There were alarms and triumphs on the tour. In Vienna Richter had forgotten to send Wagner tubas and have harp parts copied; ultimately there was a shower of laurel wreaths 'for the reformer', 'the saviour of German art', 'the master of humour'. In Budapest a Richter *Flying Dutchman* in Italian and Hungarian caused consternation because of additional cymbal clashes, while a joint venture with Liszt succeeded largely through his incomparable 'Emperor' concerto. Berlin was rejoicing at the time over *The Maccabees* of Anton Rubinstein; but during a *Götterdämmerung* Immolation rehearsal with Materna, Helmholtz wept throughout.

In Leipzig they endured the vulgarity and coarseness of Schumann's *Genoveva*, while Mathilde Wesendonck thought Cosima tired and older-looking.

In 1875 rehearsals at Bayreuth, a triumph of organisation on Wagner's part and tribute to the esteem and affection in which he was held by German musicians, began on July 1. In January he had written to the singers: 'You see yourself called upon—perhaps for the first time in your artistic career—to devote your powers simply and solely to the attainment of an artistic ideal'. Lilli Lehmann, a Rhinemaiden and Valkyrie, described the high spirits during rehearsals. There were Nibelung sounds from every lodging, Nibelung greetings in every street; Fasolt, Donner, and others did war dances in sheets before their hotel; Wilhelmj, leader of the orchestra, was commissioned by Wagner to collect and buy up dogs abandoned because of a new tax. On August 1 Wagner was greeted in the theatre for the first time by combined singers and orchestra; Betz as Wotan sang 'Vollendet das ewige Werk'. The acoustics were all that had been hoped. At a final garden party Liszt played his *Legend of St Francis*.

The end of 1875 saw Wagner again in Vienna for new productions of *Tannhäuser* and *Lohengrin*. On November 2 he and Cosima sat through a Verdi Requiem under Richter, on which silence was the only possible comment; a *Carmen* was interesting as evidence of the latest French manner. Cosima heard Brahms in a piano quartet and found him 'red and raw'; Richard was not looking forward to a 'one-eyed Swedish Jew' as Tannhäuser. When it was all over Wagner wrote to the king: 'I achieved miracles there, but with a trouble I could hardly bring myself to go through again'. Angelo Neumann, the herald in *Lohengrin*, described some of the miracles, admiring Wagner as 'the greatest of managers and a marvellous character actor'. He had electrified the cast as Tannhäuser at the crossway, riveted to the spot like a graven image; he had fought a hard-pressed Telramund to a perfectly punctual death; had been a snakelike Ortrud rising from the minster steps, a rapt Elsa in the wedding procession.

While in Vienna Richter made him godfather to his daughter, Richardis Cosima Eva; and with some temerity the fifteen-year old Wolf showed him his first compositions.

At the turn of the year Wagner was asked to write an *American Centennial March* by the ladies' committee of Philadelphia; he also sent the king, whose compulsive building threatened bankruptcy, part 3 of *Mein Leben*. The *March* provided Wagner no inspiration. He needed a visual image, and all he could see was the fee, five thousand dollars. Early in February 1876 he sketched the flowermaidens tune for *Parzival*, calling it a 'Wanting to be American' album leaf. On March 2 he conducted a Vienna *Lohengrin* for the opera personnel; on his departure the chorus sang 'Wach' auf!' at the railway station and Cosima commented on the deep impression left by 'the lofty room, the dim lighting, the poor people suddenly breaking into these inspired sounds'. That same month there was the first Berlin *Tristan*, with proceeds dedicated to Bayreuth by the kaiser's order; and Cosima read in a newspaper that her mother had died.

On May 3 Wagner telegraphed to the king it was twelve years today since they first met; the king replied that it was twelve years tomorrow. At 1876 festival rehearsals Wagner sometimes complained he couldn't remember names and at one period he had to retire, 'swollen like a hippopotamus' with a tooth abscess. But his mountaineering feats over the scenery were a constant astonishment, his care for every movement and word. *Rhinegold* swimming rehearsals caused bother; Richter didn't know his tempi; the banker Feustel said every day cost two thousand marks and in three weeks they would be out of money; *Rheingold* mists were a failure because the machinist had been told to economise by the directors; the dragon's neck from London never came. Cosima smoked at rehearsals and had altercations with Professor Doepler over the costumes of Siegfried and Gutrune's women. There was too much archaeology around; too many characters resembled red Indians; Wotan's hat made him a musketeer. Indeed the performances would represent the work as little as the work represented the times.

The king came by night to attend the open rehearsals. Wagner met the train at a wayside halt and accompanied Ludwig to the Eremitage. It was their first meeting for eight years and a happy one, though Ludwig did not visit Wahnfried. He forbade all demonstrations yet seemed displeased when they didn't occur. The kaiser arrived on August 12, stayed for the first *Rhinegold* the next day and *Walküre*; he confessed surprise Wagner had achieved the festival and was saved by him from tripping over backwards during an interval. Dom Pedro of Brazil came too. There were mishaps in *Rhinegold*: Wotan lost the ring, disappeared twice into the wings during the curse, and the first scene-change was bungled so that the audience was confronted with men in shirt-sleeves. But Nietzsche, physically so racked that even brief listening was torment, produced his acute and moving *Wagner in Bayreuth*; the Wesendoncks, Mathilde Maier and Malwida von Meysenbug witnessed Wagner's triumph; Judith Gautier lent kisses and caresses as comfort. Ludwig returned for the third cycle, and Wagner set for him words from Brünnhilde's final address he had written in 1852 and since abandoned.

SLINGS, ARROWS AND SPEARS
'Never again, never again' had been Wagner's main thought during the festival; but it was the 148,000 marks debt, his cruel 'Qualhall' or hall of torment, which prevented a repetition in 1877. The festival had made its effect; Karl Marx complained he was everywhere bombarded with the question 'What do you think of Wagner?' Richard and Cosima left for Italy in mid-September. They had a final meeting with Nietzsche in Sorrento, where there was talk of *Parzival*; a reunion in Rome after sixteen years with Princess Wittgenstein (St Peter's seemed a failed palace of the Caesars); and a Florence encounter with Jessie Laussot, now Jessie Hillebrand and much busied with local music. Back at Bayreuth Cosima quoted Wagner in her diary for 25 January 1877: 'I am starting *Parzival* and shall not give it up till it is

66

finished'. By the end of January the main problem left was how the spear should be won back. On April 2 Richard read Act 1 of the poem; on April 14 Act 2 was ready for Cosima: 'That is our secret, from me to you'; and on April 20 the text was complete.

By now it had been decided to attack the festival debt by giving concerts in London. Richter and Wagner were to share the conducting and the original plan was twenty Albert Hall concerts. Richard was seasick; most of the orchestra came to Charing Cross; and as usual the whole of Israel seemed to be against them. The concerts were reduced to eight, the agents were near bankruptcy, and the Albert Hall echo was in its prime. The young Bernard Shaw described Wagner's 'tense neuralgic glare' at the players, the sudden upward jerk of the baton, 'as if by a sharp twinge of gout in his elbow', and the often scrambling start. Richter was more genial with the orchestra, and the venture proved a *succès d'estime*, making seven hundred pounds for Bayreuth. Wagner read the *Parsifal* poem (as it was now spelt) at Dannreuther's in Orme Square and again had an audience of Queen Victoria, at Windsor Castle. But London seemed too like Nibelheim, 'the dream of Alberich fulfilled', in dominion of the world, ceaseless activity and work, with everywhere the imprint of damp and mist.

After the financial disappointment of London, Wagner went to Bad Ems for a cure. He kept aloof from the ladies at the springs, 'fat, malevolent, indeed spiteful, but with roses in their hats', and brooded on the possibilities of a fabled America where Liszt should accompany his singing in joint recitals. There were visits from the two Mathildes and the vexing news that the *Neue freie Presse* was to publish with commentary letters to his Viennese milliner Bertha Goldwag, the source of much public ribaldry. In Bayreuth at the beginning of August Wagner arranged his workshop for *Parsifal* and Cosima heard the first sounds. For St Cosmas's day, September 27, the prelude was ready in orchestral sketch and Richard played it to Cosima. *'Parsifal* is nonsense in

67

such a time as ours', he said; but he was writing it for his wife: 'about faith in the German spirit I will say no more'. Meanwhile correspondence with Judith Gautier secured the Paris fabrics and perfumes for his bath and person that formed the *Parsifal* background. 'Do not think badly of me', he wrote at the end of 1877; 'at my age one can indulge oneself in childish things. I have three years' work at *Parsifal* before me'.

The previous July Nietzsche had sent the Wagners greetings *via* Malwida von Meysenbug: 'My best wishes to the tireless Bayreuthers (three times a day I wonder at their diligence)'. At the start of 1878 he received the *Parsifal* poem inscribed 'To his dear friend Nietzsche, from Richard Wagner, higher ecclesiastical councillor'. Nietzsche's first reaction was to consider the text more Liszt than Wagner, a product of the counter-reformation; his second was to send in April the aphoristic *Human, all-too-human* in which he struck at the root of the matter: 'Every master has only one pupil—and that one becomes untrue to him—for he too is meant for mastership'. Cosima ascribed the later vitriolic tone of Nietzsche's Wagnerian writings to the frantic headaches at the 1876 festival; Wagner diagnosed Nietzsche's condition thus: 'a long-threatened but not unexpected catastrophe has come upon him'. Nietzsche blamed Wagner's characteristic lack of generosity for the bad reception of his book at Wahnfried.

In February 1878 the *Bayreuther Blätter* began to appear under the editorship of Hans von Wolzogen; originally intended as adjunct to a Wagnerian music school, it was now a Wahnfried house journal. After the nine volumes of prose works Wagner himself felt he had little new to say. *Parsifal* progressed well, and he arranged for eventual Munich performance in return for royalties on his other works. He knew he had never composed in such congenial circumstances and thought of going straight on to *The Victors*. He was in high spirits: Amfortas and Titurel were 'his two pharaohs' (he had been thinking of Rossini's *Moses*), and he was going to have the grail knights shuffle off at the end of Act 1 to the *Radetzky March*. Fidi sang Klingsor in the garden; Richard, like a flower maiden, would often greet Cosima with 'Du—Tor!'; the Kundry-Parsifal scene was going to be a canon; Kundry should sing a Boieldieu aria about the pleasures of travel after cursing Parsifal. For Cosima's 1878 birthday the prelude had been played by the Meiningen orchestra (they had practised it at double speed); on 25 April 1879 the orchestral sketch was complete. Richard had chest pains the following day, but they celebrated. Cosima fell asleep over coffee, and he left her a note: 'Dear wife! Rest quietly'.

'You are the complete Wahnfried, and I am your Wahnfritz', he told her. But his health was precarious. There were days when he spat blood, had stabbing in his chest, and had to be monosyllabic; 'I have a mouse which scratches round my heart, my lungs, my liver', he complained. As Richard sat watching the sunset, Cosima watched him. Liszt was now often at Wahnfried; evenings were spent at whist, with Cosima finding it impossible to play against Richard or see him in a dilemma without helping. A score card has survived inscribed by Wagner 'Everybody won'. On 28 August 1879 to honour Goethe's 130th birthday Liszt played the *Faust* symphony. Wagner was moved at Liszt's modesty concerning his own achievement and admitted with splendid cheerfulness he had himself 'stolen so much from the symphonic poems'. Bach had now joined Beethoven among favourite composers for evening music, with Richard making up words or stories for fugue tunes, and sometimes dancing.

In September 1879 Wagner wrote his open letter on vivisection to Ernst von Weber, founder-president of the Dresden society for the protection of animals. He lashed out at the experimenters who said howling dogs made less noise than a music school, and at the scientific jokes played on animals who could only take them seriously. The teachings of Darwin and Christ were linked in his mind. After a recurrence of his skin trouble (he called himself 'Rhodonasilos Tithonos', the rosy-nosed dawn), they left on December 31

69

for ten months in Italy. Naples had the worst winter in living memory, but Vesuvius was active 'making coffee for the devil'. *Mein Leben* was completed by the end of April; and a lengthy treatise, *Religion and art*, finished in July, recommended orderly migration to South America, a warmer climate where meat-eating might be unnecessary. The suggestion was followed by Nietzsche's brother-in-law, Bernhard Förster, who committed suicide in his Paraguay colony called Nueva Germania. At a reading of the *Oresteia* in June Richard wished Thyestes had been a vegetarian so that the whole dreadful story needn't have happened.

A Russian artist friend of Henry James's, Paul Zhukovsky, joined the Naples circle, found favour, and began *Parsifal* sketches. An expedition to the Palazzo Rufolo at Ravello provided the original of Klingsor's garden, and during August and September the Siena cathedral, where Fidi did some drawings, came to stand for the hall of the grail castle. The Wagner bed in the Villa Torre Fiorentina had once slept Pope Pius VI; Richard thought it large enough for a whole schism as well. There was an appalling tantrum in Venice when the family failed to find a gondola and Cosima was told: 'I must let him rage, it was a necessity, he was like Othello whom Desdemona's innocence made the more furious'. At the end of October they were in Munich, already fortified by Ludwig's agreement that *Parsifal* should be done only in Bayreuth. There was much Wagner to be heard: a *Dutchman* that caused tears of emotion; a private *Lohengrin* in the royal box with Ludwig; a *Tristan* 'never listened to so sorrowfully'. On November 12 Wagner had another tantrum after directing the *Parsifal* prelude for Ludwig, when the king requested in addition the prelude to *Lohengrin*. This was their last meeting.

Back in Bayreuth Wagner was ill and irritable, calling himself 'the plenipotentiary of decline'. He had 'all the rivers of hell in his nose', Styx, Acheron, and the rest. Work on *Parsifal* scoring advanced slowly as he pondered the equivalent in sound of 'layers of cloud, which scatter and form again'. An essay *What boots this knowledge?* from the end of 1880 enshrines the view he had expressed to the Bayreuth banker Feustel: 'My hopelessness for Germany and its condition is absolutely total'; Bismarck's Reich had apparently to show her teeth in all directions 'even if it leaves her with nothing to chew'. *Know thyself* of early 1881 reverted cantankerously to the Jewish question and suggested that the Nibelung ring in the form of a cheque book now completed the eerie vision of the spectre in charge of the world.

He was convinced those in the Hofgarten must think he was drunk when he had to rest against every tree during a walk. But the grave in the garden was ready. Initially the mayor had been startled at the idea till Richard explained with what serene calm he and Cosima faced eternal rest. 'At our burial the closing scene of *Tristan und Isolde* will be played', they thought. Watched over by a pine tree from Tribschen, Eva and Isolde were found sitting there looking for worms for the tortoises, and the dog Marke demonstrated his prowess by jumping over it with a bad leg. Despondent about the future of German culture, Wagner imagined a ballet would be danced there one day, while Albert Niemann was convinced they would sell Wahnfried and the inscription on the grave would eventually read 'Here lies Meyer Cohn'.

Sadness that *The Ring* could not be repeated at Bayreuth was mitigated by the extraordinary ambition of Angelo Neumann. On impulse he had attended the second *Ring* of 1876 and immediately wished to mount the work himself. Persevering through tortuous negotiations, Neumann put together a Leipzig *Ring* in April and September 1878. Richter telegraphed to Wagner: 'Magnificent! Neumann has done marvellously!' Wagner called it the battle of Leipzig, 'the most important victory I have ever won'. In May 1881 Neumann took *The Ring* to Berlin. The Wagners attended the first cycle, for which steam was pumped from a nearby distillery, where the manager's son was an ardent Wagnerian. They returned with the family and Count Arthur Gobineau for the fourth cycle. The ovation in presence of the emperor was spoilt by Wagner's sudden departure from the stage. He

71

claimed to have had a heart spasm; Cosima's diary, mentioning laughter in the carriage home, suggests a fit of pique. Neumann was hurt, but developed a touring company to take *The Ring* as far as London in 1882, and Russia.

Gobineau, a retired diplomat met originally in Venice, had developed theories about the races of mankind which greatly interested Wagner and influenced his *Herodom and Christendom* of September 1881: 'The yellow races traced themselves back to monkeys, the white to gods'; yet the blood of Jesus might redeem all from the corruption wrought by Jewish 'cannibals now trained to be the business agents of society'. But the picture of a handsome Nubian made Wagner wonder whether the white races were not descended from the black. The summer of 1881 was otherwise spent in *Parsifal* rehearsals directed by Hermann Levi, the Jewish conductor from Munich whom Wagner wished to convert to Christianity. Levi wrote of Wagner in warmest terms to his father, chief rabbi of Giessen: 'posterity will recognise that Wagner was as great a man as he was artist, which those close to him know already'.

Liszt came again that autumn and entertained them with a tale of English people singing 'We belong to the Temperance Society' to a tune from *Norma*. Richard was heard humming 'We belong' in the moonlight, and 'We belong' provided the text for Liszt's new year greetings telegram. When Judith Gautier stayed, Wagner would excuse himself from his devoted 'hurricane': 'Ma chère enthousiaste, prenez pitié de moi'. But Bayreuth weather was a general discouragement. Summer and winter were exactly the same, and 'the trees only become green from boredom'. When he took a walk, the air barked at him; he would sell Germany to the French and go to Sicily on the proceeds. There were thoughts of a Nile cruise, abandoned for fear of stomach upsets; and during October Cosima reserved rooms in Palermo.

The pills Wagner took for the sea voyage acted as 'agents provocateurs', but their first Sicilian task was the freeing of trapped birds. *Parsifal* Acts 1 and 2 were now fully scored and on November 8 Act 3 was started. Wagner lamented that in Siena he had ruled the pages wrongly and bewailed his compulsion to make the score itself a work of art: 'It is terrible to have pedantry and genius in the same bag'. Work was not quite up to schedule and for her birthday Cosima received, 'pia fraus', the Parsifal score with last page complete but a gap in front of it. He continued in the new year, with much exhaustion on the day Parsifal climbed the steps to the consecration table; and on January 13, while Joseph Rubinstein was playing excerpts from Die Feen to the family, he slipped out to write the final notes. 'Es ist vollbracht!' Cosima wrote in her diary. The next day Renoir called. Richard suggested somebody should paint Cosima in the garden of Eden offering Wagner the apple of vegetarianism. Instead Renoir produced what he called 'a small reminder of this marvellous head', and Wagner considered 'like the embryo of an angel, swallowed as an oyster by an epicure'.

In March he had a bad heart attack: 'My entrails have tied themselves in knots lest they forget something'. Cosima's only comfort was that she had fainted instantly: perhaps in the end they would die together. During a brief April visit to Venice, Richard got the band in St Mark's Square to play the Thieving magpie overture and complained about the lack of humour in the Bayreuther Blätter. After securing a floor in the Vendramin palace for the autumn, they returned to Bayreuth.

ES IST VOLLBRACHT
Kent's question in King Lear, 'Who's there, besides foul weather?' cheered him up for Parsifal rehearsals. He now considered Shakespeare his 'only spiritual friend' and had written as Richard III to London for a special Parsifal gong: 'My kingdom for a tam-tam'. His assistants Humperdinck and Rubinstein reminded him of Rosencrantz and Guildenstern. One evening Cosima tried on the Kundry costume; first impressions about the dresses in general were terror,

73

unbridled amusement, anxious care to alter them. The transformation music for Act 3 was too short; after various adjustments, additional bars by Humperdinck were accepted. The first performance was on 26 July 1881, with Wagner's particular pleasure in the flowermaidens. He would shout bravo at them and be hissed for it; during a reception he sat by the stove with them and joked. Carrie Pringle, the only English flowermaiden, seems to have stirred his emotions; she alone was not asked back the following year. It was a grievous blow that Parzival-Ludwig did not attend, but at the end Cosima felt they should be pleased. In spite of much exhaustion during the performances, Wagner conducted from the Act 3 transformation to the end on the last night. A difference in the orchestral playing was noticed, and from the pit he bade his artists farewell.

It had been painful saying goodbye to the dogs; Wagner was convinced he would not see Marke again. On the train to Venice in September Cosima wrote letters and Richard commented: 'You want to ensure only your coffin is followed when we die'. In St Mark's Square he liked to sit between the pillars of the cathedral portal like Hagen on watch. He looked back with pleasure to the *Parsifal* performances and thought they were now living 'just like Jews', with no idea where they would be next. Neumann's advocacy of *The Ring* was a constant wonder: 'How strange it had to be a Jew'. And when Gobineau died in October, 'his only contemporary', he played the Siegfried funeral music. For Cosima's birthday there was a performance in the Fenice Theatre of the youthful symphony he had written fifty years before. It was reconstructed by Anton Seidl from orchestral parts, since Mendelssohn had never returned Wagner the score he sent him.

On that occasion Liszt played too, amused that the lagoons of Venice seemed to have strengthened Richard's wit. Wagner in his turn complained of Liszt's 'turbulent sleepiness', calling him 'King Lear' and his adherents the hundred knights. He talked to Cosima about his own main weaknesses, rudeness and the love of soft fabrics in lustrous colours. Their medical adviser, Dr Keppler, was encouraging about both of them in January; they thought they would never die and made plans for Richard's hundredth birthday. He added Schröder-Devrient to his dreams about former women in his life and commented: 'All my womenfolk are going by me!' Five days before he died he sang loudly: 'Don Giovanni, tu m'invitasti', and during his last evening he played the lament of the Rhinemaidens. On 13 February 1883, the day of his fatal heart attack, he was working on an essay *Concerning the feminine principle in human affairs*. Cosima could not be separated from the body for twenty-five hours. King Ludwig, when the first paroxysm of grief was over, summed up what was in some measure a joint achievement: 'I was the first to recognise the artist whom the whole world now mourns'.

Books in English about Wagner

On his way to Paris in 1839, Wagner's London included the House of Lords; as Philharmonic conductor in 1855 he reached the pages of *Punch*; but London saw no Wagner opera till 1870, when *Der fliegende Holländer* was produced at Drury Lane in Italian. New York followed a year later with *Lohengrin*, while Germany was already halfway through *The Ring*. The theories had been partly expounded and mocked in London, but Dannreuther's *Richard Wagner, his tendencies and theories* of 1873 was the first serious study. Yet in the decade to Wagner's death London experienced with horror and delight all the operas from *Rienzi* to *Götterdämmerung*. By the end of the century the Liszt correspondence had appeared in English (1888), Ashton Ellis's periodical *The Meister* (1888-95) had flourished, the prose works were translated, Shaw had written *The perfect Wagnerite* (1898) and Ernest Newman *A study of Wagner* (1899).

PROSE WORKS

Wagner's intentions seemed always misunderstood; hence his need to explain and justify. He needed also to chart for himself the course he felt opera should follow. Wagner first planned a collected edition of his writings in 1868, sketching the contents of a projected ten volumes on 26 April. The first edition of a differently ordered ten volumes came 1871-85; a sixth edition (Leipzig, 1914) extended the series to sixteen volumes.

William Ashton Ellis's English version excluded most of the poems and was published in eight volumes as *Richard Wagner's Prose Works* (Kegan Paul, Trench, Trübner, 1892-9; reissued NY, Broude, 1967; Scholarly Press, 1972). Ellis wrestled hard with Wagner's knotted theoretical prose; the result is an English style that is *sui generis*. But Ellis's persistence has allowed the English reader to sample the full range of Wagner's mind and the depths of his thought. With all his faults, Ellis remains essential.

Volume 1 (1892) is titled 'The Art-Work of the Future etc' and includes the 'Autobiographical sketch' of 1843 and most of the Zürich treatises as far as the 'Communication to my friends', with the exception of the formidable 'Opera and drama', which makes up volume 2 (1893). In volume 3 (1894), 'The Theatre', is the controversial 'Judaism in music', tributes to both Spontini and Spohr, instructions on the performance of *Der fliegende Holländer* and *Tannhäuser*, comments on the Nibelung project, and suggestions for the reorganisation of the theatres in Zürich and Vienna. Volume 4 (1895) is called 'Art and Politics' and includes the Vaterlands-verein speech; 'On state and religion', Wagner's theoretical firstfruit for King Ludwig; the 'German art and German policy' articles that came shipwreck in 1867 because of their anti-French feeling; the essay 'On conducting'; and heartfelt obituaries for Rossini and Ludwig Schnorr von Carolsfeld.

Volume 5 (1896) contains under the title 'Actors and Singers' writings from winter 1870 to spring 1873: such as the comedy in the antique manner, *A capitulation*; reminiscences of Auber; the 'Beethoven' essay for the 1870 centenary; 'The destiny of opera'; letters inspired by the Bologna *Lohengrin* of 1871; Wagner's defence of Nietzsche for *The birth of tragedy out of the spirit of music*; the Bayreuth speech delivered at the laying of the foundation stone. In volume 6 (1897) there appear under 'Religion and Art' many of the late essays written for the *Bayreuther Blätter*: assessments of the Bayreuth *Ring* and *Parsifal* festivals; last thoughts on poetry, music, and drama; a powerful letter to Ernst von Weber, 'Against vivisection'; and dispirited observations in such essays as 'Shall we hope?'; 'Religion and art'; 'Know thyself'; 'Herodom and Christendom'; 'On the womanly in the human race', the essay Wagner was busy with at his death. Volume 7 (1898) reverts to Wagner's early Paris writings, when youthful exuberance and the need to sell his wares kept his style fresh and disciplined. Also included are Dresden pieces on the homecoming of the dead Weber and the reorganisation of the Saxon national theatre; the pseudo-history of 'The Wibelungen' and the 1848 outline of 'The Nibelungen myth as sketch for a drama'. In volume 8 (1899) were issued the 'posthumous' writings. These included such pre-Parisian journalism as Wagner's Bellini article and 'On German opera'; a revolutionary article for Röckel's *Volks-blätter*; the scenario for *The Saracen woman*; and, most telling of all, the plan for Wagner's play *Jesus of Nazareth*.

Two of Wagner's toughest treatises have useful alternative versions in English. Edwin Evans senior translated 'Opera and drama' (Reeves, 1913) in two carefully annotated volumes, with numbered paragraphs and an analytical index for quick reference. Yet meaning remains elusive. Oliver Strunk's *Source readings in music history* (NY, Norton, 1950) has produced an abridged translation of 'Das Kunstwerk der Zukunft' which is a distinct improvement on Ellis. Wagner had five sections; Strunk offers only parts of three. Among the smaller essays Dannreuther produced a challenging 'Music of the future' in 1872. His translation of 'Beethoven' came out in 1880 (Reeves), and his 'On conducting' (Reeves, 1887) was reprinted in 1977 by Longwood Press.

There have been a number of anthologies in English using Wagner's prose works. In 1875, with a second edition in 1909, appeared E L Burlingame's *Art, life and theories of Richard Wagner selected from his writings* (NY, Henry Holt), including the 'Autobiographical sketch', 'A pilgrimage to Beethoven', 'An end in Paris', continuing *via* such later Parisian articles as 'The music of the future' and the account of the 1861 *Tannhäuser*, to the laying of the Bayreuth foundation stone. The translation is a pioneer American effort. In *Wagner on music and drama* (NY, Dutton, 1964, reissued 1977; Gollancz, 1970), the editors Albert Goldman and Evert Sprinchorn disappointingly use Ellis's translations. The book is divided into eight sections covering such topics as the cultural decadence of the nineteenth century, the Greek ideal, the origins of modern opera, Wagner's development, Bayreuth, politics. The aim is to make Wagner's thought accessible and coherent. Charles Osborne's *Richard Wagner: stories and essays* (Peter Owen, 1973) makes some emendations to Ellis for the sake of clarity, but not enough. The selection includes the best of the Paris pieces, 'Jewishness in music', and the Wibelungen essay. More successful is *Wagner writes from Paris* (Allen & Unwin, 1973), with new translations by Robert Jacobs and Geoffrey Skelton of the thirteen most important pieces among Wagner's twenty-five early despatches from Paris. The translation goes some way towards catching Wagner's youthful flair.

AUTOBIOGRAPHICAL WRITINGS
Wagner began his autobiographical jottings in August 1835. He wrote them in the Red Book, of which only four pages now survive, taking the story to September 1839; these were first published in the *Allgemeine Musik Zeitung* in 1936 and appear also in volume one of the *Sämtliche Briefe* (Leipzig, VEB Deutscher Verlag, 1967). There is no English translation. Similar jottings dealing with the period from Easter 1846 till the end of 1867 were copied into the Brown Book in February 1868; a later continuation completed the 1868 record, and with the start of 1869 Cosima began her diary, chronicling Wagner's life till the evening before he died. The Brown Book, started in August 1865 and continuing till April 1882, contains also intimate communications to Cosima, drafts and final versions of some prose works, and the sketch for a one-act comedy about a seedy theatrical troupe. *Das Braune Buch* was first published in 1975 (Zürich

and Freiburg, Atlantis); an English translation is forthcoming.

On the basis of the notes in the Red Book Wagner fulfilled Heinrich Laube's request for the story of his life till the departure from Paris in April 1842. The 'Autobiographical sketch', first published in February 1843, is lively, succinct and pithy; English translations appear in Burlingame(p. 78) and in volume one of the Ellis prose works (p. 77). An idiomatic modern translation can be found in *Wagner: a documentary study*, compiled and edited by Herbert Barth, Dietrich Mack and Egon Voss (Thames & Hudson, 1975).

In the 1851 *Communication to my friends*, also in Ellis's volume one, the Zürich exile emphasises the connection between his art and life; he sketches his development as poet and thinker since *Der fliegende Holländer* and outlines his transition from opera to drama with the *Ring* project.

The autobiography begun in 1865 at king Ludwig's request and completed in 1880 as far as the royal rescue, was dictated to Cosima and only privately printed during Wagner's lifetime. It appeared publicly under Wahnfried auspices in 1911 as *Mein Leben*, and an authorised English version came out the same year: *My life* (Constable, reissued by Scholarly Press, 1972). The virtues of this two-volume autobiography are its candour and overall accuracy; but Wagner's reputation took a hard knock when it was finally seen he had followed his own laws rather than those of a German or indeed English gentleman. A blistering attack on the English version was made by David Irvine in *Wagner's bad luck: an exposure of 800 errors in the authorised translation of Wagner's autobiography* (Watts, 1911); the errors were due to university men who neither knew Wagnerian facts nor were interested in Wagnerian subjects. In 1912 Irvine returned to the assault with *The Badness of Wagner's bad luck: a first exposure of anti-Wagnerian journalism* (Watts); this was mainly a spirited onslaught on Newman for his article on the autobiography in the *Fortnightly Review* of July 1911, plus an exposure of hypocrisy in the church of England. A first authentic edition of *Mein Leben* was published by Martin Gregor-Dellin in 1963

(Munich, List); there is no English translation.

A final piece of autobiographical writing, 'The work and mission of my life' was published in the *North American Review* for August 1879; Cosima's diary entry for 1 May 1879 makes clear that the essay was in fact by Hans von Wolzogen; Wagner corrected it that morning, found it immature, and eventually signed it.

LETTERS

The Wagner correspondence, when completely published, will total about 5000 items. In Germany there have been two attempts at the complete letters: the first started in 1913, but with no access to the Wagner family archives, and reached only July 1850; in 1967 there appeared with full Wahnfried approval the first volume of a new *Sämtliche Briefe* (Leipzig, VEB Deutscher Verlag), edited by Gertrud Strobel and Werner Wolf. Its three volumes have covered 669 letters including fifty six not previously printed, and reached May 1851. In English there is nothing comparable.

In 1927 there came out Wilhelm Altmann's selection from the letters in a translation by M M Bozman, *Letters of Richard Wagner* (Dent; NY, E P Dutton). Its purpose was to supplement *Mein Leben* by giving most coverage to the post-1864 letters, its inevitable weakness the fact it could use only Wahnfried approved versions. There is no such inhibition to a volume published first in English (Gollancz, 1951; reprinted by Vienna House, 1972) and two years later in German: *Letters of Richard Wagner: the Burrell collection*, edited by J N Burk. The collection put together mainly during the 1890s by the Hon Mrs Mary Burrell contained 840 items. Herself convinced that Cosima was a villainess, she secured the confidence of Natalie Bilz-Planer, Minna's daughter, who was of the same view, and obtained choice items from the Minna legacy. Nine letters of 1835, for instance, fired off on successive days to get Minna back from Berlin, show Wagner the lover writing, desperate, imperious. Another collection outside the Bayreuth net is *The Nietzsche-Wagner correspondence* of 1922 (Duckworth), translated by Caroline V Kerr. The snag here is the unscrupulous editing by the philosopher's sister Elisabeth Förster-Nietzsche, whose respect for documents was subordinated to her personal view of her brother's place in history. Of singular displeasure to Wahnfried was the publication in 1877 of Wagner's letters to Bertha Goldwag; they appeared in English (NY, Ungar, 1941) as *Richard Wagner and the seamstress*, translated by Sophie Prombaum, and date from the Munich period when Wagner was planning the silk and satin dream colours for the Briennerstrasse house, his dressing-gowns, and underwear.

The Wahnfried record of publication under Cosima is nonetheless impressive. Starting with the Liszt letters in 1887, those to Uhlig a year later, the series had produced fifteen more volumes by the end of 1911. The English record has by no means caught up.

The first to appear was the *Correspondence of Wagner and Liszt* (Grevel, 1888; reprinted by Haskell, 1968, by Greenwood, 1969, by Vienna House, NY, 1973), translated by Francis Hueffer, and reaching only the completion of *Tristan* in August 1859. As a record of encouragement and friendship between two composers, the collection has no equal. In 1890 came *Richard Wagner's letters to his Dresden friends* (Grevel; reprinted by Vienna House, NY, 1972), translated by J S Shedlock, bridging the years 1840-68. Copies of the Uhlig originals survived in the Burrell Collection, a fact allowing Cosima's editorial policy to be examined. Fischer and Heine, loyal supporters since *Rienzi*, are treated to affectionate banter and many requests.

Röckel, Wagner's companion in revolution, discussed art and politics with him as intellectual equal. *Richard Wagner's letters to August Roeckel* (Bristol, Arrowsmith; London, Simpkin, Marshall, Kent) appears to have come out in 1897 and has been reissued by AMS Press. Translation of the twelve letters is by Eleanor C Sellar, and an introduction by Houston Stewart Chamberlain sketches Röckel's influence on Wagner. To 1899 belong two volumes translated by William Ashton Ellis: *Letters of Richard Wagner to Emil Heckel* (Grant Richards), friendly signs of sympathy to the founder of the first Wagner society; and *Richard Wagner: letters to Wesendonck et al.* (Grant Richards, reprinted by AMS Press), chronicling a fundamental relationship in the Wagner saga, plus letters to Malwida von Meysenbug and Eliza Wille.

Ellis also translated the Mathilde, Minna, and family correspondence. *Richard Wagner to Mathilde Wesendonck* (Grevel, reprinted Vienna House, NY, 1972) came out in 1905, a record of Wagner's dealings with his 'muse'; extracts from the Venice diary are included. *Richard to Minna Wagner* (Grevel) appeared in 1909 (Vienna House reprint, NY, 1972) and shows Ellis firmly on Wagner's side. This correspondence is supplemented in the Burrell Collection, where Wagner's wilfulness gets full scope. The Minna letters are notably colloquial in style. *Family letters of Richard Wagner* (Macmillan, reprinted by Vienna House, NY, 1972) date to 1911 and cover 124 documents, 1832-74. More than half the letters are to Cäcilie and her husband Avenarius. Wagner strikes few attitudes, and only to Alexander Ritter, nephew by marriage, is he 'the sublime uncle'.

In 1912 there appeared *The story of Bayreuth as told in the Bayreuth letters of Richard Wagner* (Nisbet, reprinted by Vienna House, NY, 1972), translated by Caroline V Kerr. The Bayreuth banker Friedrich Feustel, receives forty five letters; Heckel of Mannheim gets thirty four, and there is some duplication with Ellis's 1899 volume; other recipients are Carl Brandt, Theodor Muncker. In 1900 Anton Pusinelli's son applied to Cosima for permission to print Wagner's letters to his father; it was refused. Hans von Wolzogen did a doctored selection in the *Bayreuther Blätter*; the fullest version so far published is *The letters of Richard Wagner to Anton Pusinelli* of 1932 (NY, Alfred A Knopf; Vienna House reprint, NY, 1972), edited and translated by Elbert Lenrow. A tribute to Wagner's ability to inspire and keep friendship, the correspondence with the Dresden doctor touches on intimate matters.

PERSONAL ACCOUNTS

Of incomparable value as a primary source, as running commentary on Wagner's vitality, and as monument to an untiring devotion are the Cosima diaries in two volumes, first published by M Gregor-Dellin and D Mack in 1976 and 1977, and translated into English by Geoffrey Skelton in 1978 and 1980 as *Cosima Wagner's diaries* (Collins).

The most distinguished of Wagner's disciples, Bülow and Nietzsche, each went their separate ways. *Letters of Hans von Bülow*, edited by du Moulin Eckart and translated by Hannah Waller (Alfred A Knopf, 1931) includes a magnificent series to Wagner ending in 1869, a Cosima group till 1881 (originally in French; she ends up as 'Madame'), and a collection to his daughter Daniela. Nietzsche's enchantment with Wagner is expressed in his first book, *The birth of tragedy out of the spirit of music*, written in 1872, revised in 1878, prefaced with a 'self-criticism' in 1886, and translated in the complete works edited by Oscar Levy, volume 1 (Allen & Unwin, 1909). The 1876 Bayreuth festival was celebrated in the fourth of the *Thoughts out of season*, 'Richard Wagner in Bayreuth', with perceptive comments on Wagner's achievement, character and significance; it appears in the complete works, volume 4 (1909). The firstfruits of the flight from Bayreuth was *Human, all-too-human* of 1878, aphorisms 'for free spirits' with few direct references to Wagner but abounding in innuendoes of revolt against his theories and attitudes (complete works, volumes 6 and 7; Allen & Unwin, 1909). In the complete works volume 8 appear the waspish productions of 1888: *The case of Wagner*, in which the Wagner disease is expertly diagnosed but unkindly treated; *Nietzsche contra Wagner*, tributes to the discoverer of 'a music without a future'; and *Selected aphorisms*, with strictures on Wagner the 'obscure and incomprehensible writer' and the suggestion he may have been a Jew. *Ecce homo*, Nietzsche's autobiographical sketches of 1888, expressing gratitude for the Tribschen days, wonder at *Tristan*, admiration for Cosima, loathing for Wagnerians, is in the complete works, volume 17 (Allen & Unwin, 1911), and in a modern version by R J Hollingdale (Penguin, 1979).

Pulverised by Wahnfried, Ellis and Newman, Ferdinand Praeger's *Wagner as I knew him* (Longmans, Green, 1892) contains much error, deliberate falsehoods, but enough vitality to have enchanted Shaw even after he realised it was more fiction than fact. Angelo Neumann's *Personal recollections of Wagner*, translated by Edith Livermore from the 1907 German original (Constable, 1909), tells an entertaining tale of business negotiations tempered with hero-worship and the near miracle by which the *Ring* became a touring success. The *Ring* costumes of 1876 were designed by C E Doepler, whose autobiography (1900) contains an enthralling Wagner chapter. A halting translation in a privately printed monograph, *A memoir of Bayreuth 1876: C E Doepler*, is complemented by eight splendid reproductions of the costume designs (P Cook, 6 Upper Wimpole St, London, 1979). Representative of the younger faithful was Hans von Wolzogen. An 1883 German essay, written at the impact of Wagner's death, was translated in 1894 by Agnes and Carnegie Simpson as *Reminiscences of Richard Wagner* (C Giesel, Bayreuth). It contains glimpses into the family circle and impressive testimonial to Wagner's mesmeric power.

Among Wagner's female admirers, the radical Malwida von Meysenbug was one of the least fair but most intelligent. An abridgment of her *Memoiren einer Idealisten* (Berlin, ?1868-76) came out as *Memoirs of Malwida von Meysenbug: Rebel in a crinoline*, edited by Mildred Adams from the translation of Elsa von Meysenbug Lyons (Allen & Unwin, 1937); it recounts how Malwida was struck by the Zürich prose works, admired Wagner as Philharmonic conductor in London, and became a devotee after some *Tristan* in Paris. Judith Gautier in *Wagner at home* (Mills & Boon, 1910), translated from *Auprès de Richard Wagner. Souvenirs 1861-82* by Effie Dunreith Massie, recounts a first pilgrimage to Tribschen and subsequent thraldom. Not all the supposed conversations can be *verbatim* and her descriptions are often more enthusiastic than balanced. Lilli Lehmann's *My path through life*, translated by Alice Seligman (Putnam, 1914), is the autobiography of a first Bayreuth Rhinemaiden and Valkyrie. She finely chronicles the trials and excitements of the 1876 festival, achieved only through Wagner's top voltage.

French admiration for Wagner dates mainly from the Paris *Tannhäuser* period, when Baudelaire among others was swept off his feet. His 1861 essay, *Richard Wagner et Tannhäuser à Paris*, translated into English as *Richard Wagner and Tannhäuser in Paris* (1964), fascinatingly details Wagner's impact on a poet's mind as man, thinker and musician. An account by Edmond Michotte of the interview he arranged between Wagner and Rossini was not published till 1906. *Richard Wagner's visit to Rossini*, translated by Herbert Weinstock (University of Chicago Press, 1968), reflects both composers in a good light. August Lesimple, founder of the Cologne Wagner society, describes in *Richard Wagner, personal recollections*, translated by Carl Armbruster (Lucas, Weber, 1884), the contradictions in his hero's character. He attended and comments on the 1877 *Parsifal* reading given for the delegates at Bayreuth. Adolphe Jullien's acquaintance with Wagnerian matters also went back to the Paris *Tannhäuser*. In *Richard Wagner, his life and works*, translated from the 1886 French by Florence Percival Hall (Boston, Knight & Millet, 1900; reprinted by AMS Press, 1974), Jullien suggested that scribbling admirers had made Wagner almost unintelligible. Quieting critics by claiming Mozart had been as rude about the French as Wagner, Jullien quotes opposing sources to give a balanced picture of Wagner among his contemporaries.

CONTEMPORARY CRITICISM

The first period of Wagnerian debate may be said to end with the composer's death. In the *Lexicon of musical invective* (NY, Coleman-Ross, 1953, 2nd edition 1969, pb 1969) Nicholas Slonimsky devotes his longest section to Wagner, with characteristic extracts from James William Davison, Ferdinand Hiller and Eduard Hanslick. Literary scorn is represented by Ruskin (unforgettably), Wilde and Tolstoy, that of composers by Tchaikovsky, Strauss (full repentance later), and Rimsky-Korsakov. *From Mendelssohn to Wagner* (Reeves, 1912) was compiled by Henry Davison as a memoir of his father J W Davison, forty years critic of *The Times*. Davison wrote admirably, chose Mendelssohn, trounced Wagner in 1855, considered him subversive of true art, uncouth as a man, an erratic conductor, but magical orchestrator. Henry Pleasants III made a selection of Hanslick's criticism in *Vienna's golden years of music 1850-1900* (NY, Simon & Schuster, 1950; Gollancz, 1951), tracing his career from *Tannhäuser* enthusiasm to his description of Wagnerian opera as an art that knew only superlatives. With slight changes the anthology was reissued as *Eduard Hanslick, music criticisms 1846-99* (Penguin, 1963).

English Wagnerism owed its impetus to two German-born critics. Edward Dannreuther launched a series of essays on 'Wagner and the reform of the opera' in the *Monthly Musical Record* of 1872; they were issued in book form as *Richard Wagner, his tendencies and theories* (Augener, 1873) and expanded into a second edition as *Wagner and the reform of the opera* (Augener, 1904). A lightweight biography based roughly on the 'Autobiographical sketch' is supplemented with a sensible résumée of the theories and an admission that for many people Wagner's reputation rested on his mistakes of policy. Francis Hueffer became music critic of *The Times* in 1878. Four years previously he had issued *Richard Wagner and the music of the future* (Chapman & Hall; Books for Libraries reprint, 1971), a cursory examination of the theories and the operas then written. His *Richard Wagner* (Sampson Low, Marston, 1872, revised 1881) gives interesting details on early English performances of the operas.

There is a lively and thoughtful account of the 1876 *Ring* festival in Joseph Bennett's *Letters from Bayreuth* (Novello,

1877). Originally printed in *The Daily Telegraph*, they describe Wagner's triumph, the pretensions of his house, the scenic truth and grandeur of the stage spectacle, the tedium of Wotan and the vastly superior *Flying Dutchman*. A fusillade directed by Major H W L Hime mainly against Hueffer's 1874 book and called *Wagnerism, a protest* (Kegan Paul, Trench, 1882) examines the possibility that music may end where it began, in noise. The twenty-year old Bernard Shaw just qualified as a contemporary critic when he watched Wagner at the Albert Hall in 1877. His impressions can be found in the volume edited by Dan H Laurence as *Bernard Shaw, how to become a musical critic* (Hart-Davis, 1960; Da Capo reprint, 1978), plus also 'Bayreuth and back' and 'Wagner in Bayreuth'. There is much of point and wit on Wagner in *London Music 1888-89 as heard by Corno di Bassetto* (Constable, 1937), and a standard of journalism airily and impishly kept up throughout the three volumes of *Music in London 1890-94* (Constable, 1932). They chronicle Wagner's increasing popularity and start reviewing Ellis's versions of the prose works. The 1895 essay 'The sanity of art' deals also with Wagnerism and its undegeneracy and is reprinted in *Major critical essays* (Constable, 1932), the volume that contains also 'The perfect Wagnerite' (p. 102). There is useful gathering of Shaw's Wagner writings in an anthology compiled by Louis Crompton as *The great composers: reviews and bombardments by Bernard Shaw* (University of California Press, 1978).

ICONOGRAPHY

The best selection of Wagnerian pictures and documents has been compiled and edited by Herbert Barth, Dietrich Mack and Egon Voss (Thames & Hudson, 1975). Splendidly produced, it invites the browser to the delights of early Wagnerian productions and contains such piquant juxtapositions as Wagner and Clara Schumann on the Dresden uprising. In *Wagner, a pictorial biography* (Thames & Hudson,

1963), Walter Panofsky brings insufficient scholarship to bolster a pleasant selection of pictures. *Wagner and his world* by Charles Osborne (Thames & Hudson, 1977) is again better with illustration than text, which oddly suggests the dramas exist in spite of the theories and Wagner should have found a better librettist.

Devoted largely to the successors, *Richard Wagner in Bayreuth* (Belser, 1976) is translated from the German of Hans Mayer, with documentation by Gottfried Wagner, a great-grandson; it concentrates on the fall and redemption of the Bayreuth idea from its inception to the centenary. Guilt for Hitler and the war lies heavily on pictures and text, which has inaccuracies. In *The Wagner family albums* (Thames & Hudson, 1977), Wolf Siegfried Wagner, another great-grandchild, delves further into the woes of Wahnfried, a second house of Atreus unable to avoid the ancestral curse.

DICTIONARY, COMPANIONS
Edward M Terry's *A Richard Wagner dictionary* (NY, Wilson, 1939; Westport, Greenwood Press reprint, 1971) sets out to be 'a convenient volume of reference for the general reader' but is too inaccurate to succeed. In *The Wagner companion* (W H Allen, 1977) Raymond Mander and Joe Mitchinson have compiled cast lists, synopses, reviews of the operas to provide a lively introduction to Wagner and his theatrical achievement; Shaw on Bayreuth 1889, Millington on Bayreuth 1976 are included. A more ambitious book with the same title, *The Wagner companion*, edited by Peter Burbidge and Richard Sutton (Faber, 1979) has excellent essays from Michael Tanner on 'The total work of art', Deryck Cooke on 'Wagner's musical language', Robert Bailey on 'The method of composition'. Elsewhere the standard varies, notably in the weird bibliography. *Wagner 1976: a celebration of the Bayreuth festival* (The Wagner Society, London, 1976) is an anthology of views on Wagner by critics past and present. The book aims to reconcile

enthusiast and academic, to contrast English and German Wagnerians.

MAJOR BIOGRAPHERS
English Wagnerians were set an exacting standard by Mary Burrell in her *Richard Wagner 1813-1834*, of which 100 copies were privately printed in 1898. A book magnificent in format, it relies almost exclusively on documentary evidence squirrelled together in Germany and fully published only in 1951 (p. 81). Painstaking research into Wagner's ancestry launches a study in which few previous 'facts' are left unquestioned. The Hon Mrs Burrell had her prejudices, refusing to believe in Wagner's authorship of *Mein Leben* and attributing it to Cosima.

Carl Glasenapp produced two editions of his Wagner biography during the composer's lifetime. An enlarged version, *Das Leben Richard Wagners* started publication in 1894 and formed the basis of William Ashton Ellis's translation in the six-volume *Life of Richard Wagner* (Kegan Paul, Trench, Trübner, 1900-1908; Da Capo reprint, 1977). Like Glasenapp before him, Ellis found Wagner almost uncontrollable. By volume 3, 100 pages of Glasenapp had turned into 500 of Ellis, and with volume 4 Glasenapp's name was abandoned. At the end of volume 6 Ellis had reached only 1859, and the biography remains a splendid torso. Ellis gives Wagner the benefit of most doubts. The book is eminently readable but not quick-witted enough for its mercurial subject. Ellis produced also slighter studies. In 1887 appeared *Richard Wagner as poet, musician and mystic* (Society for the encouragement of the fine arts), succinct attempt to demonstrate Wagner's significance through the theoretical works and dramatic achievement; and in 1892 an outraged riposte with *1849: a vindication* (Kegan Paul) to Praeger's account of Wagner as revolutionist. Both are worth a dip for period preaching and period controversy.

Ernest Newman's critical mind and caustic pen worried at Wagner for more than fifty years. So searching was his

Wagnerism that the faithful thought of him for many years as an enemy. As early as 1899, *A study of Wagner* (Dobell; NY, Putnam), devoted to Wagner's practical achievements and theoretical speculations, gave no quarter. Wagner's reading of the cosmos was not a matter of universal interest nor was the musical stage suited to philosophy. If Wagner's mind was unfit for sane thinking, the theoretical baby could advantageously be emptied out with the muddied bathwater of Wagnerian prose. A small book in the Music of the Masters series, *Wagner* (John Lane, 1904), was written when the Mathilde Wesendonck letters were hot press. It touches lightly on the world theories, delights in Wagner's lapses from metaphysics towards sanity, tells the opera plots succinctly, and winds up with an excellently reasoned bibliography.

By 1914, when he produced *Wagner as man and artist* (Dent 2nd revised edition, 1942; Peter Smith reprint, 1963; pb Jonathan Cape, 1969), Newman was deep in his subject, convinced of the dichotomy between genius and man with feet of clay. *Mein Leben* had been published three years before, and Newman was in his element demonstrating its fallibility. He was prepared now to investigate the musical theory, particularly the 'Beethoven' essay, and gives proper testimony to Wagner's musical growth by examination of the early works. In 1931 Newman was goaded into producing *Fact and fiction about Wagner* (Cassell) through his double interest in Wagner and detective work, and given an admirable springboard by Hurn and Root in *The truth about Wagner* (p. 97). Newman belaboured the two Americans, throwing in for good value the 'sentimental' Finck (p. 93), the Praeger 'mixture of knavery and foolery' (p. 85), the dismissive study by Turner (p. 95), and less justifiably the honourable if blinkered Hanslick.

By the time of the four-volume biography, *The life of Richard Wagner* (Cassell, 1933-47; CUP reprint, 1977), much new material justified the undertaking. Though Newman started almost more hares than even he could chase, remitting nothing in his critical standards, he came to a more generous understanding of Wagner than hitherto. The sleuthing extends to Nietzsche, whose share of the fourth volume seems excessive till one realises the significance of Newman's plea for full publication of Cosima's diaries and Wagner's Brown Book.

Newman's most genial Wagner book was *Wagner nights* (Putnam, 1949; reprinted 1961 and 1977), published in America as *The Wagner operas* (NY, Alfred A Knopf, 1949; reprinted 1963). Newman took advantage of recently published prose sketches to produce fascinating background studies to the operas from *Der fliegende Holländer* to *Parsifal*.

Since 1977 the Red Book, Annals, Brown Book and Cosima's diaries have all been available (pp. 79, 84); Curt von Westernhagen is the first major biographer to have assessed them. *Wagner,* first published in 1968, was revised and enlarged ten years later, providing Mary Whittall with the edition for her English translation (CUP, 1978). Westernhagen sees Wagner positively as a man concentrated on his life's work, which in turn mirrored his experience. If Wagner emerges with more dignity than he needs, this is small penalty for a scrupulous and balanced account.

OTHER BIOGRAPHIES TILL MEIN LEBEN
Between Wagner's death and the publication of *Mein Leben* lay the second period of controversy, when biographers depended on Glasenapp and the 'Autobiographical sketch', plus the mounting volume of correspondence from Wahnfried. Facts were thinly spread, philosophies half understood; but the zest of discovery was there, the thrill of partisanship, the sense of great things stirring behind the Bayreuth steam curtain. Gustav Kobbé was at Bayreuth for the first *Parsifal* and remained a staunch Wagnerian. Most of his Wagner analyses have been absorbed into the perennial *Complete opera book* (p. 100); there remain the opening sections of *Wagner's life and works* (NY, Schirmer, 1890; Gordon Press reprint), containing a workmanlike biography and lively journalism on the trials of reaching Bayreuth and

the excesses of devotees. W H Hadow's 'Wagner' section in *Studies in modern music* (Seeley, 1892) is a finely written account, excellent on the 1855 London excursion, under-informed on Cosima, with a well balanced assesment of the dramas. The American Henry T Finck, critic of the *New York Evening Post*, attended the first Bayreuth *Ring*. The two-volume *Wagner and his works* (Grevel, 1893; Haskell reprint, NY, 1969) acknowledges the value of Glasenapp and Jullien but claims independence as biographer. Scorned as 'sentimental' by Newman, he tells a lively story with considerable style, advocating the works with fervour and intelligence. A modest contribution from Charles A Lidgey, *Wagner* (Dent, 1899), gives most of his space to the dramas and plots. Friendship with Wilhelmj enabled him to supplement a thin biography with a Wagner letter to the leader of the first *Ring* orchestra requesting he should rescue animals about to be destroyed because of the new German dog-tax (p. 64).

Houston Stewart Chamberlain, writing originally in 1896, had his *Richard Wagner* translated in 1897 (Dent; Philadelphia, Lippincott; AMS Press reprint, 1974). Eschewing detail and archives, Chamberlain's aim was simplicity, to reflect the image of Wagner, to give a connected account of his teaching. As Cosima's son-in-law he gives a very lopsided version of the Munich triangle and ludicrously mishandles king Ludwig. W J Henderson's *Richard Wagner* (Putnam, 1902, 2nd revised edition 1923; AMS Press reprint, 1971) is a study by an American critic of various New York newspapers enjoying the advice of Cosima and Henry Krehbiel (p. 100). The aim is expository rather than critical. The biography skirts the obvious problems, avoiding chronology when troublesome; but the sagas are investigated in depth and 426 AD is fixed as the death of Siegfried.

As polemical coda to the second period of controversy may be cited *A Wagnerian midsummer madness* (Grevel, 1899) by David Irvine. Ever ready to break a lance for the cause, the author takes issue with Newman over the prose works as representing current anti-Wagnerism, and seeks also to rout earlier enemies such as Bennett and Chorley by raising much controversial dust.

OTHER BIOGRAPHIES FROM MEIN LEBEN TILL 1939

The publication of *Mein Leben* renewed interest in Wagner and launched a third period of critical disharmony. Three distinguished German studies, each concentrating on one aspect of Wagner's career, preserve their vitality and interest. In 1912 Julius Kapp wrote on Wagner and women under the catchpenny title *Richard Wagner und die Frauen: eine erotische Biographie*; the work was enlarged in 1921 and 1929, and an English translation by Hannah Walker appeared in 1931 as *The women in Wagner's life* (Routledge). An 'authorised' translation as *The loves of Richard Wagner* (Allen) came out in 1951. Wagner's susceptibility needed little demonstration, but Kapp keeps his head amid the swirl of skirts and emphasises the central importance of Minna, Mathilde and Cosima. The thesis of Paul Bekker's *Richard Wagner: das Leben im Werke* (1924), translated by M M Bozman as *Richard Wagner: his life in his work* (Dent, 1931; reprinted by Arno and Books for Libraries, 1970; Greenwood reprint, 1971) is to demonstrate the 'elemental unity in all Wagner's life and work', and to show that Wagner's need to express himself was balanced by search for experience. The interruption to the *Ring*, the interminable sufferings, the taking of Cosima, all were aspects of life for art's sake. Woldemar Lippert, keeper of the principal public archives of Saxony, was well placed to produce in 1927 *Richard Wagners Verbannung und Rückkehr, 1849-62*, translated by Paul England as *Wagner in exile 1849-62* (Harrap, 1930; AMS Press reprint, 1974). Based on scrupulous research, it presents the background machinations that kept Wagner's pleas for clemency at bay. Whether in Zürich or Venice, he remained of considerable interest to the police.

A French account of more imagination than accuracy was

94

published in 1932 as *Wagner: histoire d'un artiste* by Guy de Pourtalès. It appeared as *Richard Wagner* in an English translation by J Lewis May (Jonathan Cape, 1932; Greenwood reprint, 1972). With sections titled 'The poet of the viewless countenance', 'Loge', 'Tristan', 'Wotan', 'Prospero', the book is lyrical and highly strung, but contains thoughtful insights.

Writers in English were overshadowed by Newman; nor did they match continental effort. John F Runciman, for instance, in *Richard Wagner, composer of operas* (Bell, 1913), thought little of *Mein Leben*, considered Schopenhauer's influence a disaster and *Parsifal* contemptible. He is nonetheless pithy and apposite on the man, independent in judgment, and won a good word from Newman. George Ainslie Hight admitted that his two-volume *Richard Wagner, a critical biography* (Arrowsmith, 1925) contained no new facts, of which the world already possessed more than enough. Though translator of Chamberlain, Hight is wary of Wahnfried, upbraids Glasenapp for 'outrageous partisanship'. Wagner's superiority, he thought, lay in his intense humanity. The composer William Wallace made two attempts on Wagner. The first came out in 1925 as *Richard Wagner as he lived* (Kegan Paul, Trench, Trübner), allusive in manner, muddled in presentation. As a trustee of the Royal Philharmonic Society, Wallace knew his stuff on the London episode of 1855; he hopelessly underestimates Wagner's booklist and considers the *Ring* less suited to the theatre than the study and concert room. In *Liszt, Wagner and the Princess* (Kegan Paul, Trench, Trübner, 1927) there is biographical high spirits and an interesting if loaded examination of Wagner's musical debt to Liszt.

W J Turner's *Wagner* (Duckworth, 1933) has little sense of proportion and a conviction that Wagner's popularity is on the wane. With small feeling for Wagner's greatness, Turner is unavoidably superficial. In 1934 Sir W H Hadow produced *Richard Wagner* (Thornton Butterworth; AMS Press reprint, 1974). Properly respectful of Mary Burrell and Newman, he gives also a spirited defence of Praeger. Once Newman's biography has run out with volume 1, errors creep in. The music is generously assessed on classical criteria. Robert L Jacobs's *Wagner* (Dent, 1935; revised 2nd edition, 1974; Littlefield reprint, 1977) remains the current Master Musicians volume. It is succinct and well proportioned, with neat summaries of the theories and consideration of Wagner's influence on the orchestra, composition, and conducting. It is an effective wonder of compression.

OTHER BIOGRAPHIES SINCE 1945
The doubts raised by Bayreuth during the Hitler period and the attitude of Wagnerian discussion in its fourth phase are most tellingly reflected in R W Gutman's *Richard Wagner: the man, his mind and his music* (NY, Secker & Warburg, 1968; 2nd edition, 1971; pb, 1974). Obsessed with 'Jewishness in music' and the race theories of the late prose works, Gutman impugns Wagner's motives at every turn. A salutary douche in many ways and a work of fine scholarship, the book is nonetheless unbalanced and ultimately tiresome. *Richard Wagner* by Hans Gal first appeared in 1963 and was translated into English by Hans-Hubert Schönzeler (Gollancz, 1976). Seeing Wagner as a Narcissus with the innocence of a wild animal, Gal has no very uplifting view of his character; nor is he prepared to take seriously all Wagner's stage creations. Alternately perceptive and exasperating, the book has stimulating ideas for friend and foe. Chappell White's *An introduction to the life and works of Richard Wagner* (New Jersey, Prentice-Hall, 1967) has concise and efficient biography, with much bizarre detail omitted. The author is better with the anti-semitism than with Wagner's Christianity. There are brief synopses of the dramas, good observations on the orchestral reforms and musical architecture.

Elaine Padmore's modest little volume in the Great Composers series, *Wagner* (Faber, 1971, 2nd edition, 1978), has a pleasant mixture of good photographs and mostly judicious if uncritical text. There are sufficient inaccuracies to sound a note of caution. John Chancellor's *Wagner* (Weidenfeld & Nicholson, 1978) is more ambitious, but sometimes muddled in presentation and naive in approach. There is evidence of recent scholarship, but it has insufficiently permeated the book. It remains an easy-going account by an obvious partisan. In *Richard Wagner, his life, art and thought* (Elek, 1979), Ronald Taylor knows well the German literary and historical background. Interesting observations result. But he has insufficient musical background to steer clear of obvious pitfalls and is not always sure of standard Wagnerian facts. Derek Watson's *Richard Wagner* (Dent, 1979) is a workmanlike biography, extended but manageable, that makes sound use of recent sources. Avoidable errors have crept in and some Newman misconceptions persist. At the Watson judgment seat Wagner's flaws tend to obscure his vitality.

ESSAYS BIOGRAPHICAL
A paper by O G Sonneck with the provocative title *Was Richard Wagner a Jew?* (Washington, 1912), reprinted from the Proceedings of the Music Teachers' National Association for 1911, examines the question whether Wagner was Geyer's son and whether Geyer was Jewish. In both cases the answer is negative. With *The truth about Wagner* (Cassell, 1930) two American journalists, Philip Dutton Hurn and Waverley Lewis Root, after limited access to the Burrell Collection, sought ham-handedly to rehabilitate Minna at Cosima's expense. The result is ludicrous history but effective propaganda.

WAGNER AND LITERATURE
Wagner's dramas and Greek tragedy by Pearl Cleveland Wilson (NY, Columbia University Press, 1919) draws parallels between the *Ring* and the *Oresteia*. Much is far-fetched, but there is food for thought in the contrast between

Aeschylus's punishment for sin and Wagner's creative sympathy with it. *Schiller and Wagner, a study of their dramatic theory and technique* by Marie Haefliger Graves (Ann Arbor, Michigan, 1938) traces Schiller's progress from drama to a form approaching opera, and expounds the mission shared by Schiller and Wagner to endow an unspoiled people with a new culture by means of the theatre. Dietrich Fischer-Dieskau's *Wagner and Nietzsche* was first published in 1974; the English version by Joachim Neugroschel came out in 1978 (Sidgwick & Jackson). A superb musician's attempt at a pair of divergent geniuses, the book keeps to well-trodden paths. If it wanders, error creeps in.

Sir Oswald Mosley's booklet on *Wagner and Shaw: a synthesis* (Sanctuary Press, 1956) evinces great admiration for both. Shaw he knew and relished for his brilliance; he indicates the main flaw in *The perfect Wagnerite* (p. 102), and considers Wagner outstripped Shaw in his conception of life's future. In *Richard Wagner and the modern British novel* (New Jersey, Associated University Presses, 1978) John Louis DiGaetani traces the influence of Wagner on Conrad, Lawrence, Forster, Woolf, Joyce. The book is impressive in intention more than achievement. There is a case, but the author treads not too lightly where angels would keep clear.

LITERARY AND PHILOSOPHICAL STUDIES

Thomas Mann, fascinated by Wagner at all stages of his career, read an important paper in 1933 for the fiftieth anniversary of Wagner's death. Translated into English as 'The sufferings and greatness of Richard Wagner' by H T Lowe-Porter in *Essays of three decades* (NY, Alfred A Knopf, 1947; Secker & Warburg, 1947), the essay examines Wagner's linking of psychology and myth, with wisdom also on his nationalism. A book of immense fascination is Jacques Barzun's *Darwin, Marx, Wagner* (Secker & Warburg, 1942; 2nd revised edition, 1950; Doubleday pb, 1958). Dealing with 'the three great prophets of our destinies', the author stresses their missionary zeal, supposed isolation, and warfare against the century. Barzun is adept at half-truths, and draws stimulating conclusions from them; ultimately Wagner is too protean for him. *The political concepts of Richard Wagner* by Maurice Boucher (NY, M & H Publications, 1950), translated from the French by Marcel Honoré, traces the steps by which Wagner the young man of the world came to view German faults as qualities, and how for him revolution turned into regeneration. Boucher sees little connection between Wagner and the Third Reich: the United Nations was more in his line. Leo Stein, however, in *The racial thinking of Richard Wagner* (NY, Philosophical Library, 1950) traces links through Wagner, Bismarck, Wilhelm II, Hitler, with Wagner prominently pitting nationalism against Judaism. The argument is more emotional than rigorous.

Bryan Magee's *Aspects of Wagner* (Alan Ross, 1968; 2nd revised edition, 1973) has telling points on Wagner's reaction to the Jewish renaissance at the opening of the ghettoes. He is admirable, too, on Wagner's characters as subjects of feeling but objects of action, on Wagnerolatry and his influence on composers and musical standards. In his *Richard Wagner* (NY, Twayne, 1969), Robert Raphael examines Wagner's achievement in devising myths that can function as metaphors for the human condition. He is acute on art and Hans Sachs, and the significance of Parsifal's redemption. H F Garten's *Wagner the dramatist* (John Calder, 1977) gives a useful survey of Wagner's development through the prose works and the dramas projected and completed. Garten's German literary background is helpful, and he covers much ground in a small space. The author died before completing the *Parsifal* chapter or dealing with the late essays.

ANALYSIS AND CRITICISM OF THE DRAMAS
The most rigorous and revealing of the nineteenth-century investigations is *The legends of the Wagner drama: studies in mythology and romance* by Jessie L Weston (David Nutt,

1896; AMS Press reprint, 1976). Her examination of Wagner's text compilation and assessment of his judgment makes excellent reading. She admires the mastery of the *Ring* text but dislikes Wagner's debasing of Brünnhilde in *Götterdämmerung* Act 2. She gives him higher marks for *Parsifal* and the originality of *Tannhäuser*. Other early treatments are less distinguished. Henry Edward Krehbiel's *Studies in the Wagnerian drama* (Osgood, McIlvaine, 1893; AMS Press reprint, 1975) is by the reviser of Thayer's *Beethoven*. There is intelligent comment, not least on *Parsifal*, which he found hard to take. He is good on *Tristan* sources and took the trouble to copy mastersongs in Nuremberg. *The music dramas of Richard Wagner and his festival theatre in Bayreuth* by Albert Lavignac was planned as a practical guide to Bayreuth for the French and translated by Esther Singleton (Nisbet, 1898; AMS Press reprint, 1970). A distinguished musicologist, Lavignac found all melody and no accompaniment in Wagner. His biography is outdated, the critical sense refreshing.

The lively Wagner section in *Kobbé's complete opera book*, revised for the ninth edition by the Earl of Harewood (Putnam, 1976) has its origins in Gustav Kobbé's *How to understand Wagner's the Ring of the Nibelung* (Reeves, c 1890; Scholarly Press reprint, 1976; AMS Press reprint, 1977) and *Wagner's music-dramas analysed* (NY, Schirmer, 1904; Putnam, 1927), dealing with the seven last operas. Passages on Wotan the bore and Wagner misunderstood are now omitted, as are many superlatives. A series of booklets by Alice Cleather and Basil Crump (Methuen, 1904-12; *The Ring of the Nibelung* reprinted by Richard West, nd, and Folcroft, 1977) tackles the operas from *Tannhäuser* to *Parsifal*. Equipped with pithy introductions that range widely without eccentricity, the main text is a brief synopsis laced with relevant Wagner quotations. J Cuthbert Hadden's *The operas of Wagner: their plots, music and history* (Jack, 1908) avoids both technicalities and certain important facts. Weird colour plates by Byam Shaw give the book a period flavour, as does the confession the author had not yet heard *Parsifal*.

The German original of Houston Stewart Chamberlain's *The Wagnerian drama* (Bodley Head, 1923) came out in 1892, hammering home the significance of Wagner the poet. The *Ring* has transferred drama into the depths of the human soul: a sunrise was now significant mainly for its effect on those watching it. Chamberlain's art tends to be more total than even Wagner's. A main interest of *Wagner's operas* (NY, Farrar & Rinehart, 1937; Scholarly Press reprint) by Lawrence Gilman, is to glimpse the American Wagner scene in the heady 1930s. There is enthusiasm, though not for *Rienzi*, and wordiness. In Gerald Abraham's *A 100 years of music* (Duckworth, 1938; 2nd revised edition, 1949; pb South West Book Services, 1974), the Wagner section examines Lorenz's ideas on Wagnerian form. Tested on Act 1 of *Die Walküre*, they create much interest and some disbelief; if applied to the whole of *Die Meistersinger*, they postulate a single 'Bar', with Acts 1 and 2 the 'Stollen', Act 3 the 'Abgesang'.

Jack M Stein, in *Richard Wagner and the synthesis of the arts* (Detroit, Wayne State University Press, 1960; Greenwood reprint, 1973), demonstrates shifts in Wagner's theory as musical experience took him beyond *Opera and drama*, catalyst of the early *Ring* operas. Schopenhauer's idea, for instance, of music as the redeeming art allowed Wagner to let rip in *Tristan*, and the later theories caught up. Stein's case is well argued. The temptation to reject Audrey Williamson's little *Wagner opera* (Calder, 1962) for biographical errors should be resisted till a number of canny and shrewd points on the dramas are absorbed. A stimulating study by Carl Dahlhaus originally published in 1971 as *Richard Wagners Musikdramen*, is translated by Mary Whittall as *Richard Wagner's music dramas* (CUP, 1979), and updated to include the Bayreuth *Ring* of 1976. Dahlhaus's aim is to assess the essentials of music drama; his achievement to mingle pointed comment and detailed investigation in less than two hundred thoughtful pages.

101

STUDIES OF INDIVIDUAL EARLY OPERAS

John Deathridge on *Wagner's Rienzi* (OUP, 1977) is a scholarly reappraisal of the work's significance from an examination of sketches and drafts. The origins in Bulwer Lytton and perhaps a Mary Mitford play are investigated, its stylistic debts, and performance problems by no means solved in the Wahnfried attempt to make *Rienzi* a music drama. Frank Granville Barker's *The Flying Dutchman* (Barrie & Jenkins, 1979) is an easygoing enquiry into the work's origins and history, with illustrations straying as far as James Mason and Ava Gardner in the film *Pandora and the Flying Dutchman*. There is a synopsis, libretto with translation, and a chronology that needs checking. Cecil Hopkinson's *Tannhäuser: an examination of 36 editions* (Tutzing, Hans Schneider, 1973) gives the tortuous publishing history of a work Wagner was constantly changing. At the end of his life he said he still owed the world a new *Tannhäuser*.

STUDIES OF THE RING

The genesis of the *Ring* is treated in two important works. 'Wagner's musical sketches for Siegfrieds Tod' is a chapter by Robert Bailey in *Studies in music history: essays for Oliver Strunk*, edited by Harold Powers (Princeton, 1968). It demonstrates the nature of Wagner's false start on the embryonic *Ring*. Certain tonalities remained fixed in Wagner's mind, but the completed *Götterdämmerung* shows the same text could foreshadow two very different settings. Curt von Westernhagen's *The forging of the 'Ring'*, translated from his 1973 *Die Entstehung des 'Ring'* by Arnold and Mary Whittall (CUP, 1976) makes good, detailed use of unpublished sketches to explore Wagner's composition process. Westernhagen propounds much of value, but the implications of the sketches are not always followed through.

On the interpretation of the *Ring* there are four outstanding studies. Bernard Shaw's *The perfect Wagnerite: a commentary on the Niblung's Ring* (Grant Richards, 1898; 4th edition, 1923; Dover reprint, 1966) fastens on Wagner the enemy of capitalism and Siegfried as superman. Hence Shaw looks askance at the reversion to 'opera' in the last four acts of the *Ring*, where Wagner seems to abandon philosophy for preaching. Thomas Mann's 'Richard Wagner and the *Ring*' translated by H T Lowe-Porter in *Essays of three decades* (NY, Alfred A Knopf, 1947; Secker & Warburg, 1947), was originally given as a Zürich lecture in 1937. It sees Wagner's achievement as the German equivalent of the monumental novel writers in other countries, resulting in 'perhaps the loftiest, most compelling art the century has to offer'. In *Wagner's 'Ring' and its symbols: the music and the myth* (Faber, 1963; revised 2nd edition and pb, 1969) Robert Donington approaches Wagner by way of his symbols, using the modern tools of depth psychology. Wagner's knowledge of human problems enabled him to create rounded characters for the stage while himself failing to adapt to the realities of life. A study by Deryck Cooke, *I saw the world end* (OUP, 1979), would have been a splendid contribution had the author lived. In the event he barely had time to demolish his predecessors and hint at the criteria he proposed for a rigorous musico-dramatic analysis of *The Ring*. But the calibre of Cooke's mind is clear with less than a quarter of the book done.

Selected Wagner writings on the *Ring* were put together in two parts by Sebastian Röckl, published by Breitkopf & Härtel, and translated by Constance C Parrish. In 1907 appeared *What does Wagner relate concerning the origin of his Nibelungen poem and how does he interpret it?*, based on letters of Liszt, Röckel, Uhlig, with extracts from prose works and sketches for *Siegfrieds Tod*. *What does Richard Wagner relate concerning the origin of his musical composition of the Ring of the Nibelungs?* came out in 1908 with a broad selection of letters plus the 1872 dedicatory poem to Ludwig II. A recent anthology on the work, *Penetrating Wagner's Ring* edited by John Louis DiGaetani (New Jersey, Associated University Presses, 1978), brings together relevant material from Wagner himself and authors as diverse as Shaw and Andrew Porter. In the introduction DiGaetani spends too much time proving the *Ring* a comedy.

Among specialised treatments, a quixotic broadside by David Irvine is called *Wagner's Ring of the Nibelung and the conditions of ideal manhood* (Grevel, 1897). He deals energetically with the *Jesus of Nazareth* sketch, parasitical Jews, the work's tribute to nature, and Wagner's merit in having stated the problem of life even if he failed to solve it. John Schuler's *The language of R Wagner's Ring des Nibelungen* (Lancaster, Pennsylvania, Steinman & Foltz, 1909) is weak on biography but informative on Goethe's significance as librettist, Wagner's skill in getting saga into drama, his vocabulary and statistics on *Stabreim*. *Woman characters in Richard Wagner: a study in 'The Ring of the Nibelung'* (NY, Nervous and Mental Disease Publishing Co, 1924) by Louise Brink examines Wagner's message to the unconscious life of the folk, the vicissitudes of woman's development in the *Ring*, and Wagner's apparent assumption that the Oedipus situation is a natural one.

Three general studies of the *Ring* are worth cautious perusal. L Archier Leroy in *Wagner's music drama of the Ring* (Noel Douglas, 1925) has woodcuts by Paul Nash and considers the plot in detail. If the brief biography is unreliable, there is sound sense on Wagner as man of the theatre. A scanty Appendix B lists the *Ring* records available at the time. Aylmer Buesst's *Richard Wagner: the Nibelung's Ring* (G Bell, 1932; 2nd edition 1952) follows the plot and music act by act. The work of a conductor, the book is descriptive rather than interpretative. 'Weaving' and 'Splashing' appear among the 112 motif titles. Musically Buesst keeps his head; historically less so. The virtue of *A musical guide to the Richard Wagner Ring of the Nibelung* (NY, Simon & Schuster, 1940; AMS Press reprint, 1973) by Ernest Hutcheson, eventually president of the Juilliard School, lies in a simple telling of the tale and page by page references to the Schirmer scores. It is good to know the bear trots home to the inversion of the Siegfried motif.

Among innumerable pocket guides to the *Ring* it may be worth mentioning the earliest one, Hans von Wolzogen's *Guide through the music of Richard Wagner's Nibelungen*, translated by N H Dole (NY, G Schirmer, nd). The labelling of the 90 motifs caused Wagner himself some doubts, but there is room also for a smattering of Wahnfried philosophy and such period pieces as Wotan's 'strong, majestic Alarum song' to Erda. In *The musical design of the Ring* (The Musical Pilgrim, OUP, 1926) A E F Dickinson concentrates on the 70 most important themes and attempts to grade them in order of significance by totalling their appearances. Apparently under the impression that in *Rheingold* scene iii Alberich turns into a mouse, Dickinson has a small-scale view of the work.

STUDIES OF TRISTAN UND ISOLDE

Joseph Kerman's searching essay 'Opera as symphonic poem' in *Opera as drama* (NY, Alfred A Knopf, 1956; pb Random Press) sees Wagner's work as religious drama rather than tragedy and has telling points on the concentration of the 'action' in Tristan's soul, with its climax in the delirium scene. *The first hundred years of Wagner's Tristan* (NY, Columbia University Press, 1964) was charted by Elliott Zuckermann. The author examines the genesis of the work, its impact on Nietzsche, the symbolists and French composers, novelists such as Lawrence, d'Annunzio and Mann, and the theorists of atonalism. The dangers of Tristanism are examined with caution and some irony.

STUDIES OF DIE MEISTERSINGER

Three *Meistersinger* studies may be cited in ascending order of importance. Cyril Winn's competent little guide, *The Master-Singers of Wagner* (The Musical Pilgrim, OUP, 1925) analyses the work concisely with page references to the Schott scores and a sufficiency of music examples. No axes are ground. In a delightful study of *Wagner and Wagenseil* (OUP, 1927), Herbert Thompson, himself a lawyer,

105

traces Wagner's pleasure in the ancient 'doctor and professor of law' who wrote about the mastersingers in Latin, and presented a silver chain and gilt medallion to the guild. At much greater length in *Wagner and Die Meistersinger* (OUP, 1940) Robert M Rayner covers Thompson's ground as well as dealing with all stages of the work's creation. There is enough biography nor too much theory; it makes a genial and stimulating study.

STUDIES OF PARSIFAL

The most wary and entertaining writing about *Parsifal* comes from Claude Debussy in *Monsieur Croche anti-dilettante* (1921). There is an idiomatic translation in Richard Langham Smith's *Debussy on music* (Secker & Warburg, 1977). Of four modest guides, the earliest is *Wagner's Parsifal* by Francis Hueffer (Schott, 1884), a sensitive attempt at analysis of a work at once fascinating and baffling. The author notes with pleasure the shrinking of a *prima donna* to Wagner's quadrisyllabic Kundry in Act 3. In David Irvine's *Parsifal and Wagner's Christianity* (Grevel, 1899; AMS Press reprint, 1974) much is made of the contrast between the primitive simplicity of Wagner and the clergy-ridden complexity of contemporary Christianity. Irving is neither dull nor level-headed. Charles T Gatty's *The sacred festival-drama of Parsifal by Richard Wagner* (Schott, 1894) tells the story in the manner of an ancient lay, reprints Wagner's programme note for king Ludwig, and gives a literal prose translation of the text with reference to the musical themes. The work is interpreted in orthodox Christian terms. In *Parsifal* by Charles Cantor (Year Book Press, 1914) the muddled British public is asked to distinguish between Holy Communion and the love feast in readiness for the first British performance of the work. There are sensitive references to Dante in connection with Amfortas, some good points on the symbolism, and a tribute to Wagner's spiritual generosity.

TRANSLATIONS AND RECORDING

To say the Wagner poems are virtually untranslatable neither exaggerates their literary value nor underplays the special problem of getting a singing text from one language into another. Yet two English translations have made recent history. The version of *The flying Dutchman* translated by Brian Large and Peter Butler (Duckworth, 1975) was used for the first television production of a Wagner opera in November 1975. The illustrations show that for this occasion Daland's ship was a paddle steamer and the spinning chorus had factory background. The grammar of the translation is sometimes rough and ready; but it has speed and salty vigour. The first complete recording in English of a Wagner opera (p. 131) used the text of *The Ring: English translation* by Andrew Porter (Dawson, 1976; pb Norton, 1977), which also usefully discusses the complexity of the problem and its literature. Familiar from the London Coliseum production, the version makes immediate sense, jars seldom, and fits the music with words that may lack Wagnerian resonance but are always apt.

The first complete recording of *The Ring* is chronicled in John Culshaw's *Ring resounding* (Secker & Warburg, 1967; NY, Viking Press, 1967). Events grave, such as the substitution of a new Siegfried after three sessions, and gay, such as the transport of kippers to Vienna for Ljuba Welitsch, characterised the seven-year venture, which taxed to the full the resources of those with faith in it.

BAYREUTH AND WAGNER PRODUCTION

An important source book for the way Bayreuth might have gone is Adolphe Appia's *Music and the art of the theatre*, translated from the French of 1898 by Robert W Corrigan and Mary Douglas Dirks (University of Miami Press, 1962). Appia saw the first *Parsifal*, and in reaction sought to substitute for painted scenery the subtleties of lighting. His theories were scorned at Bayreuth till 1951. Fleeting glimpses of the Cosima and Siegfried festivals between 1901 and 1908 can be found in Rose Koenig's *Three impressions of Bayreuth* (Reeves, 1909), an unpretentious little book. Even then the Bayreuth orchestra seemed a marvel to a Londoner, and the female Wagnerian a mixture of defiant virtue, severity, and pity for all others. *The Ring at Bayreuth and some thoughts on operatic production* by Victor Gollancz (Gollancz, 1966) is discursive to a fault and pronounces pompously on the work and Wieland Wagner's 1965 production. Enthusiasm peeps through, for other composers more than Wagner; Wieland provides a graceful *envoi*. A shrewder assessment can be found in Geoffrey Skelton's *Wagner at Bayreuth: experiment and tradition* (White Lion, 1965; 2nd revised edition, 1976), which succinctly characterises each of the theatre's directors. If the accolade is given to Wieland and Wolfgang, their claim is carefully argued. A superficial and chatty account of *New Bayreuth* by Penelope Turing (Jersey Artists, 1969; 2nd revised edition, 1971) mingles the magic mountain with Bamberg, the Bibiena opera house and the Begum. But the sequence of festivals from 1951 to 1970 comes pleasantly alive.

THE WAGNER FAMILY
Hans Jachmann's account of *Wagner and his first Elisabeth* (Novello, 1944) outlines with anecdotes the distinguished career of Johanna Wagner as singer and actress. She came to Dresden for *Tannhäuser*, sang Fidès in Meyerbeer's *Prophète* and Brünnhilde in Dorn's *Die Nibelungen*. The climate of her relationship with Wagner was variable, but she took part in the Bayreuth Ninth of 1872, and was Schwertleite and First Norn in the 1876 *Ring*. The *Cosima Wagner* of Richard Count du Moulin-Eckart (Alfred A Knopf, 1930), translated from the 1929 German edition by Catherine Alison Phillips, was planned as a monument to the greatest woman of the century. Amid the slightly stilted pages is fascinating material, including much from the Cosima diaries. It is significant and exasperating that the hagiographic account stops with Wagner's death. Alice Hunt Sokoloff's biography, *Cosima Wagner*

(NY, Dodd, 1969; Macdonald, 1970), also peters out with Wagner. It is an efficient, journalistic tale, making the most of its gallery of characters. *Heritage of fire* by Friedelind Wagner and Cooper Page (NY, Harper, 1945; Greenwood reprint, 1974; published in England as *The royal family of Bayreuth*, Eyre & Spottiswoode, 1948) starts with the conviction that Wagner would never have been a Nazi and goes on to chronicle the impact of Hitler on Bayreuth and the Wagner family, and the *Götterdämmerung* rows between Friedelind and her mother Winifred. A compulsive story about a great madness. In *Wieland Wagner, the positive sceptic* (Gollancz, 1971) Geoffrey Skelton recounts with obvious sympathy how the Wagner grandsons rescued Bayreuth from the Nazi taint with a style of production allusive and symbolical. In reaction against Cosima's 'definitive' Wagner, Wieland uncluttered the works and developed the use of lighting as commentary to the stage action in counterpoint with the orchestra.

Editions of Wagner's music

BREITKOPF COMPLETE EDITION

A complete edition was launched by Breitkopf & Härtel in 1912. The editor was Michael Balling, a Bayreuth conductor who succeeded Richter at the Hallé. He died in 1925, and the tenth volume in the uncompleted series came out in 1926. Much early Wagner appeared for the first time, but the series suffered from too hasty publication, insufficient sharing of the editorial burden, and deficient scholarship. The edition has been reprinted by Breitkopf in seven volumes. It is divided into three categories: Musikdramen; Jugendopern; Musikalische Werke.

In the first category appeared vol 3, *Tannhäuser* (1923), originally planned in two volumes, one to contain the Paris version of 1860-1, the other the first Dresden version of 1845 plus the modifications of 1847. Ultimately, for reasons of time and cost, a single volume came out, taking as basis the Paris version (though the abbreviated overture runs straight into the Venusberg scene in accord with Wagner's latest practice of 1875 in Vienna), with earlier versions in an appendix. Vol 4 is *Lohengrin* (1914), printed complete but with indication of Wagner's cut in Act 3. *Tristan und Isolde* (1917) came out as vol 5.

In the second category is *Die Hochzeit* as vol 12, first edition (1912) of the Introduction, chorus and septet, the only numbers set in 1833 of a libretto disliked by Wagner's sister Rosalie (p. 13). *Die Feen* appeared as vol 13, first edition in full score of a work posthumously performed at the Munich Court Theatre (1888) under Levi, who also arranged the vocal score (p.119). Vol 14 is *Das Liebesverbot* (1922), first full score of the comic opera submerged until 1972 (p.127) after its hilarious première in 1836 at Magdeburg (p.14).

The third category produced four volumes: all Wagner's completed *Songs* are in vol 15 (1914). Those printed for the first time are the *Seven compositions for Goethe's Faust* (1831); *Was du hier siehst* (German version of *Tout n'est qu'images fugitives*, written in 1839); the tenor aria extension composed in 1833 for insertion in Marschner's *Der Vampyr*; the bass aria (1837) to words by Karl von Holtei for inclusion in Karl Blum's singspiel *Marie, Max und Michel*; and the bass aria (1840) for Orovisto in Bellini's *Norma*. The volume is made up with *Der Tannenbaum* (1838), the French songs of 1840, the *Gruss seiner Treuen an Friedrich August den Geliebten* (1843) in a version for voice and piano, and the Wesendonck songs of 1857-8.

The *Choral works* of vol 16 (1913) number such first editions as a version with brass accompaniment of the 1843 male chorus performed at the unveiling of a statue to King Frederick Augustus I (*Gesang zur Enthüllung des Denkmals Sr. Majestät des hochseligen Königs Friedrich August der Gerechte*); the welcome Wagner devised for his Dresden sovereign in 1843 on his return from England (*Gruss seiner Treuen an Friedrich August den Geliebten*) and set for male chorus; Wagner's male-voice tribute to Weber of 1844 (*An Webers Grabe*); and the festival work for men's voices and orchestra, *Das Liebesmahl der Apostel* (1843).

In vol 18 (1917) are the major orchestral works: the *Faust* overture in its 1855 version (the main changes since 1840 indicated in the introduction); the *Huldigungsmarsch* of 1864 as composed for military band; the *Kaisermarsch* (1871) including the final 'Volksgesang' in honour of the new emperor; the *Grosser Festmarsch* (1876) to celebrate the American centennial; and the *Siegfried Idyll* of 1870.

Vol 20, with introduction by Balling dated 1922 but

appearing only in 1926, contains first editions of the Concert overtures in D minor (1831) and C (1832); the *Trauersinfonie* on themes from *Euryanthe* (1844) written for Weber's reburial in Dresden; and the Adagio for clarinet and strings now known to come from a work by Heinrich Joseph Baermann. Also included are the Symphony is C (1832) as reconstructed by Anton Seidl (p. 74) and Wagner's arrangement for solo violin and small orchestra of the fifth Wesendonck song, *Träume* (1857).

SCHOTT COMPLETE EDITION

The project was launched in 1970 in association with the Bavarian Academy of Fine Arts. The general editor is Carl Dahlhaus. The series is planned for at least twenty volumes in large format, with the longer operas subdivided by acts, and at least ten volumes in smaller format containing documentary sources.

Vol 3 Rienzi

Edited by Reinhard Strohm and Egon Voss in five parts (1974–   ), the volume deals with the formidable problem of producing an acceptable *Rienzi* score. The autograph is missing (given to Ludwig II, it passed eventually to Adolf Hitler), and the Dresden theatre score used for the première was also a war casualty. Acts 1-5 have been printed as parts 1–4 of vol 3 in accordance with scores copied under Wagner's supervision at Dresden in 1842-3 and now at Hamburg and Eisenach; part 5 will contain all *Rienzi* passages cut between the first performance and the making of these scores, passages that appear in Wagner's composition draft but not in Carl Gustav Klink's piano score made from the autograph and published in 1844, and passages Wagner composed later, usually shorter alternatives to sections cut since 1842.

Vol 14 Parsifal

Act 1 is edited by Egon Voss and Martin Geck, Acts 2 and 3 by Egon Voss as vol 14, parts 1-3 (1972-3). Based on the only original source, Wagner's autograph in the Richard Wagner Archive, Bayreuth, the edition notes in the critical

112

commentary at the end of part 3 the variants between MS and the first edition (1883), which appeared too late for Wagner to pass.

Vol 17 Klavierlieder

This volume, edited by Egon Voss (1976), contains the twenty songs for voice and piano already printed in the Breitkopf complete edition plus two 1840 fragments, *Extase* and *La tombe dit à la rose*, printed for the first time. The editorial preface and different versions of the Wesendonck songs indicate the increase of knowledge and scholarly rigour since Balling (1914). A series of forty nine relevant documents, from the years 1831-78, clarifies the background.

Vol 18 Orchesterwerke I

Early orchestral works up to the Symphony in C (1832) are here edited by Egon Voss (1973). Documents on their composition and performance launch the volume with fifty four sources, 1830-83. Published for the first time are an E minor fragment (possibly part of the missing *Bride of Messina* overture); two entr'actes which may originally have been part of the *König Enzio* music, a first version of the D minor concert overture and of the Symphony slow movement. Also included are the final version of the D minor concert overture, the C major concert overture, *König Enzio* overture, and Symphony in C.

Vol 19 Klavierwerke

The piano works are edited by Carl Dahlhaus (1970). The introduction notes the loss of some early pieces including a transcription or paraphrase of 'Wotan's farewell' sent as an album leaf to the Grand Duchess of Baden in 1857. The Polka for Mathilde Wesendonck (1853) is a first edition. The rest of the volume divides into early works such as the B flat sonata, Polonaise for piano duet (p. 123), Fantasia in F sharp minor, and Sonata in A; and more mature occasional pieces such as the *Album leaf* for E B Kietz, the *Album sonata* for Mathilde Wesendonck, the Zürich *Vielliebchen-Walzer* to please Mathilde's sister ('dedicated to Marie of Düsseldorf by the best dancer of Saxony known as Richard

113

the waltzmaker'), Princess Metternich's album piece, Countess Pourtalès's 'Die Ankunft bei den schwarzen Schwänen' (Arrival at the black swans), and Betty Schott's *Album leaf in E flat*.

Vol 23 Rienzi documents and texts

A selection of two hundred and eighty five documents edited by Reinhard Strohm (1976) traces the history of *Rienzi* from its first stirrings in 1836 to a letter of 1876 about cuts in a proposed Italian performance. The second part illustrates the development of the libretto.

Vol 29, 1 Ring documents

Werner Breig and Hartmut Fladt (1976) have selected five hundred and four documents to outline the composition of *The Ring* and span the years 1837-76; a second volume will deal with text variants.

Vol 30 Parsifal documents

Edited by Martin Geck and Egon Voss (1970), two hundred and forty one documents are quoted ranging from Wagner's first study of the material in 1845 to his 1882 essay of gratitude after the first series of performances. *Parsifal* texts show the literary development from the first prose sketch of 1865 to the first edition of the poem in 1877, noting also variants between the poem and the 1883 full score. The 1882 performers are listed, there are Anton Schittenhelm's notes on the first performance, an account of Wagner's changes during rehearsal as recorded by Heinrich Porges and Julius Kniese, photographs of the first performance and facsimiles of various drafts.

FACSIMILES

A main pleasure of Wagner study is the quality of his musical handwriting, meticulous, even and clear, such that a conductor could readily rehearse and perform from a facsimile score. Three complete operas were produced in facsimile by Drei Masken Verlag, Munich: *Tristan und Isolde* (1923); *Die Meistersinger* (1922); *Parsifal* (1925). The same publishers produced also the Prelude to *Meistersinger* Act 1

(1923) and *Siegfried Idyll* (1923). The *Kinderkatechismus zu Cosels Geburtstag* (Children's catechism for Cosima's birthday) came in its 1874 version (p. 63) from Schott (1937). More recently VEB Deutscher Verlag, Leipzig, has issued the *Lohengrin* prelude to Act 1 and introduction to Act 3 (1974) and the Wesendonck songs (1962), both with commentary by Heinz Krause-Graumnitz.

OTHER EDITIONS

Publishers' names are given in full except for the following:

B&H	= Breitkopf & Härtel	OUP	= Oxford University Press
Dur	= Durand		
Eul	= Eulenburg	Sch	= Schott
Fürs	= Fürstner	WVP	= Wiener Philharmonischer Verlag
Kal	= Edwin F Kalmus		
Nov	= Novello		

FULL, STUDY, AND MINIATURE SCORES OF THE OPERAS

The *Hochzeit* fragments, *Die Feen*, and *Das Liebesverbot* were not published in Wagner's lifetime and have since appeared only in the B & H complete edition (pp. 110-111). The major works were issued by three main publishers. *Rienzi*, *Der fliegende Holländer*, and *Tannhäuser* were part of Wagner's sad publishing venture with C F Meser of Dresden (later Müller and then Adolf Fürstner, Berlin). By 1852 Wagner was a force to be reckoned with; Breitkopf & Härtel of Leipzig were ready to publish *Lohengrin*, with *Tristan* following almost by instalments from Wagner's pen. Schott of Mainz took over with *Meistersinger*, in spite of sore financial trials at Wagner's hands, and remained faithful for *The Ring* and *Parsifal*.

Die Feen. Overture by A de Almeida (Heugel).

Das Liebesverbot. Overture (B & H).

Rienzi. For editorial problems see p. 112. From the time of the Dresden performance of 1858, Wagner's wishes were usually avoided. Cosima Wagner, Felix Mottl and Julius

Kniese prepared a version based on original sources but zealous to make *Rienzi* a music drama before its time (Fürs, 1897), with text in German, English (J Pittman), and Italian; miniature scores from Fürs, WVP, Eul.

Overture (Meser, Fürs, B & H, Lafleur, WVP, Eul, Broude, Luck Music).

Der fliegende Holländer. The opera has always been printed in three acts, though it was Wagner's original intention and is Bayreuth practice to give it without break. First edition (Meser, 1844) with original ending to overture and opera; Wagner's revisions (Meser, 1877), by F Weingartner (Fürs, 1897), with German, English (Paul England) and Italian (Alberto Giovannini); reprinted Broude and Kal; miniature scores from Fürs, WVP, Eul by Max Hochkofler. As *Le vaisseau phantôme* (Dur, 1897), with German, and French by Charles Nuitter.

Overture (B & H, Meser/Fürs, WVP, Eul, Boosey, Broude, Luck Music).

Tannhäuser. This is editorially the most complex of the Wagner operas. First edition (Meser, 1845) was a lithograph of the composer's MS. Wagner's abbreviations and alterations after performance, mainly to the Act 3 introduction and ending, were engraved by B & H and published by Meser/Müller (1859). This score was reissued (Fürs, c1880). English by Mrs John P Morgan and Italian by Salvatore de C Marchesi added (Fürs, 1903), reprinted Broude and Kal; by F Mottl (Peters, 1925) follows Fürs 1903 for vol 1, with five Wagner revisions as vol 2 (Peters, 1972 has the Bacchanale and other inserts in sequence). Miniature score by Hochkofler (Eul, 1929) has German and Nuitter's French, with six variants as supplement. The B & H complete edition (1923) runs the overture straight into the Bacchanale (as Wagner did in 1875 at Vienna) and follows the vocal score by Joseph Rubinstein (Fürs, 1876; see p. 120). A full score with Nuitter's French (Dur, 1891) separates overture and Bacchanale (as in the 1861 Paris performances) and claims to be 'conforme aux exécutions modèles de Bayreuth' (1891, under Cosima).

Overture (Fürs, B & H, Broude, Kal, Eul by Hochkofler, WVP, Boosey, Ricordi); Bacchanale in orchestral version (Fürs, Broude, Kal, Eul by Hochkofler); Bacchanale with chorus parts (Dur); overture shortened and running into Bacchanale (Fürs); introduction to Act 3 in original extended form (Nov), in shortened form (Fürs, Dur, B & H, Eul by Hochkofler); Arrival of guests at Wartburg, March (Kal).

Lohengrin. First edition (B & H, 1852), German only; miniature score (B & H, 1906) with German, English of H and F Corder, French of Nuitter; German only in complete edition (B & H, 1914); German only (Peters, 1917); followers of trilingual B & H 1906 (WVP, Eul by Deryck Cooke, Broude, Kal).

Act 1 prelude (WVP, Broude, Kal); Act 3 introduction (B & H, Broude, Luck Music); Act 1 prelude and Act 3 introduction together (Eul, Boosey); Procession to the cathedral (Kal).

Tristan und Isolde. First edition (B & H, 1861), German only; Germany with English of H and F Corder, French of A Ernst, L de Foucard, P Brück (B & H, 1904-5), reprinted Broude, Kal; by F Mottl, German only (Peters, 1914), reprinted Dover; miniature scores following B & H 1904-5 (WVP, Eul).

Act 1 prelude with Wagner's concert ending (B & H, Eul, Boosey); prelude and Liebestod (B & H, WVP, Eul, Boosey, Ricordi, Kal).

Die Meistersinger. First edition (Sch, 1868), German only; by Richard Sternfeld in two vols (Peters, 1914), reprinted Kal; miniature scores (Sch, Eul) have German, English of Frederick Jameson, French of A Ernst.

Act 1 prelude with concert ending (Sch, B & H, WVP, Eul, Boosey, Ricordi, Broude, Luck Music; Penguin by Dyneley Hussey and Gordon Jacob); Act 3 prelude (Sch, B & H, Eul, Broude); preludes to Acts 1 and 3, dance of apprentices, procession of masters, greeting to Sachs (Sch); Act 3 prelude, dance of apprentices, procession of masters (B & H, Kal).

Der Ring des Nibelungen. First edition of the four scores

(Sch, 1873-6), German only, reprinted Kal; by F Mottl (Peters, c1910), Germany only, *Die Walküre* reprinted Dover; miniature scores with German, English of F Jameson, French of A Ernst (Sch, Eul).

Excerpts from the cycle: from *Rheingold*, Entry of the gods into Valhalla (Sch, B & H, Boosey, Broude, Kal); from *Walküre*, Siegmund's love song (Sch, Eul), Ride of the Valkyries (Sch, B & H, Eul, WVP, Boosey, Ricordi, Broude, Kal), Wotan's farewell and magic fire music (Sch, Eul, Broude, Kal); from *Siegfried*, Forest murmurs (Sch, B & H, Eul, Broude, Kal); from *Götterdämmerung*, Siegfried's journey to the Rhine with Humperdinck's ending (Sch, B & H, Lengnick, Kal), Siegfried's funeral march (Sch, B & H, WVP, Eul, Broude, Kal).

Parsifal. First edition (Sch, 1883), German only; Peters, German only, reprinted Broude, Kal; miniature scores (Sch, Eul) with German, English of Margaret H Glyn, French of A Ernst.

Act 1 prelude with concert ending (Sch, B & H, WVP, Eul, Boosey, Ricordi, Broude, Kal); Act 1 transformation and final scene (Sch, Eul, Kal); Good Friday music (Sch, B & H, WVP, Eul, Broude, Kal).

VOCAL SCORES OF THE OPERAS IN COLLECTED SETS

A composite edition covering *Rienzi* to *Parsifal* from the original publishers with German text (Fürs representing Meser, B & H, Sch, 1903-10). *Rienzi*, largely following the 1844 vocal score, *Der fliegende Holländer*, including the later endings to overture and Act 3, *Tannhäuser*, following the 1859 full score, are by Gustav F Kogel (Fürs); *Lohengrin* and *Tristan* by Otto Singer (B & H); *Meistersinger, The Ring* and *Parsifal* by Karl Klindworth (Sch).

B & H produced an edition of the operas (1912-22) from *Das Liebesverbot* to *Parsifal* under the title 'Sämtliche Musikdramen', mainly by Singer, except for *Lohengrin* by T Uhlig and *Tristan* by R Kleinmichel; English translations were by Ernest Newman, except for *Das Liebesverbot* by

Edward J Dent (which has also French by Amédée and Frieda Boutarel), *Rienzi* by Fanny S Copeland, *Lohengrin* by H and F Corder; the German is revised by W Golther. The works have introduction, contents, and motif analysis by Carl Waack. For *Rienzi* Singer had access to the Dresden theatre full score; *Der fliegende Holländer* uses Wagner's latest thoughts; *Tannhäuser* follows the Meser/Fürs vocal score by Joseph Rubinstein (p.120).

Schott published the works from *Rienzi* to *Parsifal* in various editions. All were done by K Klindworth, with piano part sometimes simplified, English translation usually by F Jameson. *Rienzi* had English by John Bernhoff and followed the Dresden première score; the *Dutchman* with later overture and ending used Bernhoff's English; *Tannhäuser* follows the Meser/Fürs vocal score by J Rubinstein (p. 120); the English for *Parsifal* was by Margaret H Glyn. In addition the scores from *Meistersinger* to *Parsifal* were issued in another simplified version by Richard Kleinmichel with English from H and F Corder.

A Peters edition of 1914 covers *Der fliegende Holländer* to *Parsifal*, with German only. The scores are mainly by F Mottl, though the *Dutchman* was by Gustav Brecher (incorporating hints from Wagner's essay *Bermerkungen zur Aufführung des Fliegenden Holländers*); *Tristan* by F Mottl and G F Kogel; *Meistersinger* by G F Kogel. The *Tannhäuser* follows the full score of 1859.

A set from G Schirmer in German and English ranges from *Der fliegende Holländer* to *Parsifal*. Scores by August Röckel (*Dutchman*, in the Dresden version); Natalia Macfarren (*Tannhäuser*, following the Dresden full score of 1845); Uhlig (*Lohengrin*); R Kleinmichel (*Tristan*); K Klindworth in simplified version (*Meistersinger, Ring* and *Parsifal*). English versions by J Troutbeck and T Baker (*Dutchman*); Natalia Macfarren (*Tannhäuser*); Stewart Robb (*Lohengrin* and *Parsifal*); H G Chapman (*Tristan*); F Jameson (*Meistersinger* and *Ring*).

119

Die Feen. By Hermann Levi (Heckel, Mannheim, 1888), in German.

Rienzi. First edition by C G Klink (Meser, 1844), German only; by Klink (Dur, 1869), with French by Nuitter and J Guilliaume; by T O Cesardi (Ricordi), with Italian by Arrigo Boito.

Der fliegende Holländer. First edition by A Röckel (Meser, 1844), German only; Dresden version, by J Pittman (Boosey), English adaptation of John P Jackson; with later changes, by F Brissler (Meser/Fürs); by Berthold Tours (Nov), with English of J Troutbeck.

Tannhäuser. First edition by Wagner, his only vocal score for one of his own works (Meser, 1846, for the first version, 1852 for the second), German only; by Macfarren and with her English text (Nov, 1872), a first vocal score based on the 1859 full score; by Brissler (Meser/Fürs, c1885) in German only; with English translation by Paul England (Boosey, 1900), both after the 1859 full score; by E Vauthrot (Flaxland, Paris, 1861), with Nuitter's French, first edition of the Paris version; by J Rubinstein (Meser/Fürs, 1876), first edition of the version running overture and Bacchanale together and incorporating Wagner's latest thoughts; by T O Cesardi (Ricordi, c1890), with Italian of Salvatore de C Marchesi, this reverts to the Wagner vocal score of 1852; by Robert Keller (Fürs, c1892), with English of Mrs John P Morgan, based on Rubinstein's vocal score; by E Vauthrot (Dur, Schoenewerk, Paris, 1891), with Nuitter's French, again separating overture and Bacchanale and claiming to follow 1891 practice (p. 116).

Lohengrin. First edition by T Uhlig (B & H, 1851), German only; by Berthold Tours (Nov), with English of Macfarren and German below; by Sir Arthur Sullivan and Josiah Pittman (Boosey), with English by John Oxenford, Italian and German; by T Uhlig (Kal), with English of H and F Corder, reprint of the B & H edition.

Tristan und Isolde. First edition by Hans von Bülow (B & H,

1859), German only; the same with English by H and F Corder (B & H, 1882); by R Kleinmichel, also in simplified version (B & H, 1885), and with English by the Corders (c1890).
Die Meistersinger von Nürnberg. First edition by Karl Tausig (Sch, 1867), with prelude arranged by Bülow, German only.
Der Ring des Nibelungen. First edition by K Klindworth (Sch, 1861-1875); by R Kleinmichel (John Church, Cincinnati), with preface and English version by Henry T Finck.
Parsifal. First edition by J Rubinstein (Sch, 1882), German only; by O Singer (Goossens, Brussels, 1914), with French by Judith Gautier and M Kufferath, issued to commemorate the Brussels première; no editor (Nov, 1919), with English of C Aveling; by G van den Dyck (Boosey, c1948), with English by Edward Teschemacher.

CHORAL WORKS
Das Liebesmahl der Apostel for men's voices and large orchestra. First edition of full score (B & H, 1884), German only; with English of F Corder and French of E Destranges (B & H, 1892); miniature score (Eul), with English by F Corder, French by M Kufferath; vocal score by E Bianchi (Lucca, Milan, c1875), with Italian of Arrigo Boito as *La cena degli apostoli*; no editor, and with anonymous English as *The holy supper of the apostles* (Nov).
An Webers Grabe for male chorus. Score (E W Fritzsch, Leipzig, 1872).
Kinderkatechismus for children's voices and small orchestra. Composed in 1873 for voices and piano, orchestrated in 1874; with facsimile of the MS and piano reduction by F June (Sch, 1937).

SONGS
Collections
Sämtliche Lieder by Emil Liepe (B & H), based on Balling's complete edition, including the *Faust* settings, *Tannenbaum*, French and Wesendonck songs; *Zehn Lieder aus den Jahren 1838-58* by Wolfgang Golther (Drei Masken Verlag, Munich,

121

1921), contains *Der Tannenbaum*, four French songs, as well as the Wesendonck set.

Separate songs and sets

Der Tannenbaum. First edition by August Lewald in *Europa* (Leipzig, Stuttgart, 1839).

Trois mélodies ('Dors, mon enfant', 'Mignonne', 'Attente'). First edition by August Lewald in *Europa* (Leipzig, Stuttgart, 1841-2); reprinted (Dur, Schoenewerk, Paris, 1870); in German of F A Leo as 'Schlaf ein, holdes Kind', 'Die Rose', 'Die Erwartung', with French also (Fürs, 1871).

Dors, mon enfant. With English of Francis Hueffer (Sch, 1876); with English of R H Elkin (Boosey, 1897).

Les deux grenadiers. First edition, financed by Wagner (M Schlesinger, Paris, 1839), French only; reprinted with French and German text (Sch, 1843), to Wagner's annoyance; also (Brandus, Paris, 1848).

Gruss seiner Treuen an Friedrich August den Geliebten. First edition of the version for solo voice and piano (Meser, 1844).

Adieux de Marie Stuart. First edition (*Revue musicale*, May 1913).

Wesendonck songs. (i) original version for voice and piano, first edition (Sch, 1862), with German only; with English of A C Bunton (Sch, 1899); with English of F Hueffer (Sch, 1883); by A Randegger, with English of F Mansfield (Nov, 1910), with English of E Newman (B & H, 1912); with English of Grace Hall (G Schirmer, 1914). (ii) with orchestral accompaniment by F Mottl and Wagner, first edition (Sch, c1910); later edition (B & H); reprints (Kal, Luck Music); *Träume*, no. 5, in Wagner's arrangement for violin solo and small orchestra, with voice part included as alternative (Schott, c1910); see also p. 123.

ORCHESTRAL MUSIC

König Enzio, Polonia, Christopher Columbus, Rule Britannia overtures. First edition by F Mottl as 'Vier Ouvertüren' (B & H, 1908).

Symphony in C. First edition, based on A Seidl score and

Wagner's corrections (Brockhaus, Leipzig, 1911); reprinted Kal.

A Faust overture. First edition of revised version (B & H, 1855); reprinted Broude and Kal; miniature score by E Praetorius (Eul).

Träume. No. 5 of the Wesendonck songs (p. 122), arranged by Wagner for solo violin and small orchestra (Sch, 1878).

Siegfried Idyll. First edition (Sch, 1878); reprinted Broude and Luck Music; later editions (B & H, WVP, Eul, Boosey, Ricordi, Penguin by Dyneley Hussey and Gordon Jacob); see also facsimiles, p. 115.

Huldigungsmarsch. (i) original version for wind band, first edition (Schott, 1871); (ii) arrangement for full orchestra by Wagner and Raff (Sch, Eul).

Kaisermarsch. With concluding 'Volksgesang' (Peters, 1871, Eul).

Grosser Festmarsch (American Centennial March). First edition (Sch, 1876); later edition (B & H, reprinted Luck Music).

PIANO MUSIC

Original works. Sonata in B flat, first edition (B & H, 1832). *Polonaise* for piano duet, first edition (B & H, 1832); since reprinted (B & H, G Schirmer, Curwen by T A Johnson); arrangement for two hands (B & H). Two-hand sketch for the *Polonaise*, first edition by Arthur D Walker (Nov, 1973). *Fantasia* in F sharp minor, first edition (C F Kahnt, Leipzig, 1905). *Grosse Sonata* in A, first approximate edition by Otto Daube (Hans Gerig, Cologne, 1960); another edition (Peters). *Album leaf* for Ernst Benedikt Kietz: 'Lied ohne Worte', first edition by F Gotthelf (J Eberle, Vienna, 1911), *Der Merker*, Jg.ii/25, 1006. *Album sonata* for Mathilde Wesendonck, first edition (Sch, 1878), later reprinted. *Züricher Vielliebchen-Walzer*, first edition as supplement to *Die Musik*, i/20-21. *Album leaf* in C for Princess Metternich, first edition (E W Fritzsch, Leipzig, 1871). *Album leaf* for Countess Pourtalès, 'Ankunft bei den schwarzen

Schwänen' (Arrival at the black swans), first edition (Fritzsch, 1897). *Album leaf* for Betty Schott, first edition (Schott, 1876).

Liszt arrangements. Liszt Complete Works, transcriptions vol 1, 'Wagner' (B & H, reprinted Gregg): Fantasia on motifs from *Rienzi*; Spinning song from *Der fliegende Holländer*; *Der fliegende Holländer*; Overture to *Tannhäuser*—concert paraphrase; Arrival of the guests on the Wartburg (*Tannhäuser*); O star of eve (*Tannhäuser*); Pilgrims' chorus (*Tannhäuser*); Introduction to Act 3 and bridal chorus (*Lohengrin*); Elsa's procession to the cathedral (*Lohengrin*); Lohengrin's admonition; Liebestod (*Tristan*); Am stillen Herd (*Meistersinger*); Valhalla (*Rheingold*); Solemn march to the holy grail (*Parsifal*). Other editions (B & H, G Schirmer, Augener).

Transcriptions and other arrangements. By A Blassmann, *Trauersinfonie* on *Euryanthe* themes (Meser, Berlin, c1885). By Hans von Bülow, *Tannhäuser* selection for piano duet (Meser, Dresden, c1855-65); *Tristan* prelude for piano duet (B & H, c1880; Augener); *Meistersinger* prelude and assembly of the masters, for piano (Sch, 1867); *A Faust overture* for piano (B & H, 1865; Augener); *Huldigungsmarsch* for piano (Sch, 1865). By Ferruccio Busoni, Siegfried's funeral march, for piano (Ricordi). By Engelbert Humperdinck, *Parsifal* prelude for piano duet (Sch, 1883); *Parsifal*, in twelve compositions for piano duet (Sch, 1883). By Felix Mottl, *Rule Britannia* overture for piano (B & H/Metzler, 1908). By Joseph Rubinstein, *Musical pictures* for piano: Love duet from Act 2 and the death of Tristan; Siegmund and Sieglinde (Sch, c1880); Siegfried and the woodbird, Siegfried and Brünnhilde (Sch, 1877); Parsifal and the flower maidens, Good Friday music (Sch, 1882); *Siegfried Idyll* for piano (Sch, 1878), for piano duet (Sch, c1900). By Karl Tausig, *Meistersinger* prelude for piano duet (Augener); Ride of the Valkyries for piano (Sch, 1863); *Kaisermarsch* for piano (Peters, 1871).

Jeux d'esprit. Chabrier, *Souvenirs de Munich*: quadrille on favourite themes from *Tristan und Isolde* for piano duet (Costallat, 1930). Fauré and Messager, *Souvenirs de Bayreuth*: fantasy in form of a quadrille on favourite themes from *The Ring* for piano duet (Costallat, 1930). Peter Warlock, *Valses rêves d'Isolde*: two slow waltzes for piano (Thames Publishing, 1976).

ENSEMBLE MUSIC
String quartet. Gerald Abraham, Quartet movement reconstructed from the *Siegfried Idyll* and final scene of *Siegfried* (OUP, 1947).
Violin and piano. By L Auer, *Traüme*, no. 5 of the Wesendonck songs (Fischer, New York, 1911). By August Wilhelmj, Walther's prize song, paraphrase (Sch, 1878); *Siegfried* paraphrase (Sch, 1884); *Parsifal* paraphrase (Sch, 1884); reprinted as nos 28-30 of Wilhelmj's *Newly revised editions of violin music* (Sch, 1901-   ).
Brass. Three fanfares for four bugles, dedicated to the 6th Royal Bavarian cavalry regiment, by O von Pauder (M Hieber, Munich, 1933); Three fanfares arranged for four trumpets by K V Jones (Chester, 1976).

SOME ARRANGEMENTS BY WAGNER
Operatic. Auber, *Zanetta*, airs arranged for flute, violin, viola, cello (M Schlesinger, Paris, 1840); Donizetti, *La favorita*, vocal score (Schlesinger, 1840); arranged for string quartet (Schlesinger, 1841); Gluck, *Iphigeneia in Aulis*, vocal score of Wagner's arrangement by Bülow (B & H, 1885); *Iphigeneia in Aulis* overture with Wagner's concert ending (B & H, Eul); Halévy, *La reine de Chypre*, vocal score (Schlesinger, 1841); Airs from *La reine de Chypre* arranged for two violins (Schlesinger, 1845).
Church music. Palestrina, *Stabat mater* for double chorus a capella (C F Kahnt, Leipzig, 1878).

Selected recordings of Wagner's music

Wagner recordings span most of the twentieth century. During this period standards of reproduction and of orchestral playing have improved beyond recognition; many of the best voices however, could be heard in the earliest years. Voice fanciers will therefore endure discs with accompaniment only a submarine hint of the Wagner orchestra, and from a time when the issue of a Wagner opera without cuts was commercially unthinkable; whereas philosophers busy with the inner secrets of *The Ring* will prefer the LP era. Original dates of recordings are given where possible and British catalogue numbers are followed by American. Further information about rare records may be obtained from the British Institute of Recorded Sound or from the Music Division of the Library of Congress. Within the Greater London area, the Chiswick District Library has special responsibility for collecting Wagner records.

Operas

DIE HOCHZEIT, DIE FEEN, DAS LIEBESVERBOT, RIENZI
A chorus and recitative from the fragmentary *Die Hochzeit* appears as part of a privately recorded set, W 301 A-F, including also Wagner's extension to a Marschner tenor aria (p. 139), songs (p. 139), the *König Enzio* overture, and *Das Liebesverbot*.

A *Die Feen* recording stems from the Bayreuth Youth

Festival of 1967; the excerpts under André Gaillard are enthusiastic but variable and issued on Colosseum (at the Bayreuth Festspielhaus), later The Golden Age of Opera EJS 433.

Das Liebesverbot on W 301 A-F is conducted by Robert Heger (1964); recording is indifferent but the expert cast includes Hilde Zadek as Isabella, the Luzio of Equiluz, Dermota as Claudio (coupling on p. 126). A second version, more complete, competently conducted by John Bell, comes from the Bayreuth Youth Festival of 1972 on Mixtur MXT 3001-3 (Bayreuth Festspielhaus).

The *Rienzi* (1976) on HMV SLS 990 and 5-Angel SX 3818 is very professional, demonic and exhausting. The Dresden Staatskapelle is conducted by Hollreiser, with Kollo as Rienzi, Siv Wennberg as Irene and Janis Martin as Adriano. A shortened version on Top Classics H 657-8 has the Berlin State Opera Orchestra under Johannes Schüler, with Lorenz in the title role, Klose as Adriano, Hilde Scheppin the Irene.

DER FLIEGENDE HOLLÄNDER

Six complete versions may begin with Keilberth's live Bayreuth performance of 1955 on Decca Eclipse ECS 665-7 and 3-London 4325. At Bayreuth the work is done without act divisions; Weber is a powerful Daland, Uhde an edgy and dark Dutchman, Varnay's Senta authoritative. Konwitschny's German State Opera performance of 1960 on Electrola IC 149-30206/8 has worn less well, apart from Fischer-Dieskau's hypersensitive Dutchman and Frick's expressive Daland. Covent Garden's chorus and orchestra under Dorati (1962) have more spirit than finesse; George London's Dutchman inhabits an echo chamber, Rysanek is a Senta of conviction, Tozzi a bluff Daland.

Klemperer (1968) on Electrola IC 154-00104/6 pounds magnificently with the NPO and wind machine through the Dresden version; Adam is a thrilling Dutchman, Silja dramatic but light as Senta, Talvela an impressive Daland. Böhm's Bayreuth performance of 1971 on Deutsche Grammophon

2561211-3 and 3-DG 2709040 deals in breezes rather than gales; Ridderbusch is a dark Daland, Stewart an untragic Dutchman, Jones undisciplined as Senta. The Solti version (1977) on Decca D24D 3 and 3-London 13119 paints bold seascapes with the Chicago SO. Bailey's Dutchman spreads vocally, Janis Martin is a light Senta, Kollo's Erik overweight, Talvela's Daland a complete success.

Dutchman highlights from a 1944 Munich performance under Krauss come on Acanta DE 22017, with Hotter a weighty and tragic Dutchman, Ursuleac a girlish Senta. Veritas Records VM 106 preserves excerpts splendidly sung by Schorr as the Dutchman (1923-5), with a dramatic ballad from Melanie Kurt.

TANNHÄUSER

A 1930 Bayreuth version under Karl Elmendorff on Electrola IC 137-03130/2 launches half a dozen interesting recordings; Andresen is a bold Landgrave, Pilinsky a vital Tannhäuser, Müller a warm Elisabeth. Konwitschny's of 1961 on Electrola IC 153-30683/6 uses the Dresden overture and Venusberg with the German State Opera, Berlin; Schech is a seductive Venus, Hopf's Tannhäuser effortless and lyrical, Grümmer a dramatic yet tender Elisabeth, Fischer-Dieskau's Wolfram intelligent to a fault. A Deutsche Grammophon recording of 1961 under Karl Schröder on LPEM 19240-43 uses the same version and an uninspired Hess Radio orchestra; the cast cannot redeem a dullish set.

Sawallisch's Bayreuth 1962 performance on Philips SAL 3445-7 and 3-Philips PHS-3-960 switches to the Paris ballet, back to Dresden when the Venusberg voices enter; Bumbry is a powerfully possessive Venus, Windgassen's Tannhäuser under strain through hectic tempos, Silja makes an appealing Elisabeth, Greindl a commanding Landgrave. More satisfactory is Deutsche Grammophon on 2740 142 and 4-DG 27 11008 (1970), with Gerdes alertly in charge of the German State Opera, Berlin; Nilsson is imperious as both Venus and Elisabeth, Windgassen tired, Adam a magnificent Landgrave.

Most impressive of all is Solti (1971) with the Vienna PO on Decca SET 506-9 and 4-London 1438; the heady version is Paris plus, with coruscating orchestra, Ludwig's impassioned Venus, Kollo as heroic Tannhäuser, Dernesch appealing as Elisabeth.

Tannhäuser highlights appear on The Golden Age of Opera EJS 544 under Szell; Traubel is a splendid Elisabeth, Melchior in full flood as Tannhäuser, Kipnis a brooding Landgrave, Thorborg a ravishing Venus.

LOHENGRIN
The earliest of seven recordings (1947) has a Metropolitan cast under Fritz Busch on Cetra LO 24, led magnificently by Traubel as Elsa, and Melchior as an ethereal protagonist. Keilberth directed the 1953 Bayreuth performances with powerful results on Decca D12D5 and 5-London 4502; Greindl is dark and lyrical as Henry the Fowler, Uhde a dramatic Telramund, Steber richly sorrowful as Elsa, Windgassen a robust Lohengrin, Varnay dramatic as Ortrud. Less accomplished is the Schüchter version of 1953 on HMV ALP 1095-8, with the Hamburg Radio Orchestra on middling form; Maud Cunitz is a gentle Elsa, Schock a mellifluous Lohengrin. Bayreuth 1962 is represented by Sawallisch on Philips 6747 241 with unWagnerian briskness; Thomas makes a formidable Lohengrin, Silja's Elsa cannot match Varnay's towering Ortrud, Crass is an effective Henry, Vinay weighty as Telramund.

Kempe on HMV SLS 5071 and 5-Angel S-3641 (1964) has wondrous sensitivity and purity from the Vienna PO; Thomas and Grümmer are radiant as Lohengrin and Elsa, Ludwig and Fischer-Dieskau superb as the evil counterparts, and Frick makes an authoritative Henry. Leinsdorf's 1966 recording on RCA SER 5544-8 and 5-RCA LSC 6710 with the Boston SO sometimes lacks imagination; Hines is firm as Henry, Dooley has edge as Telramund, Amara's Elsa is fresh, Kónya's Lohengrin ethereal and commanding, Gorr a dominating Ortrud. In 1971 the Bavarian Radio and Kubelik produced lovely textures on Deutsche Grammophon 2720 036 and 5-DG 2713005; Ridderbusch is a resonant Henry, Stewart a dark and plausible Telramund, Janowitz a rapt Elsa, King a radiant and tender Lohengrin, Jones sinister as Ortrud.

A *Lohengrin* highlights record on The Golden Age of Opera EJS 557 has in Flagstad a solemn and beautiful Elsa, in Branzell a dark Ortrud, Maison an intelligent if tearstained Lohengrin.

DER RING DES NIBELUNGEN

The first complete *Ring* was Solti's; but earlier ones have since emerged. Everest 940477 imperfectly enshrines on eleven discs a Scala performance of 1950 under the magisterial Furtwängler; Flagstad as Brünnhilde, such Wagnerians as Hilde Konetzni, Svanholm, Lorenz, make enthralling listening and more than adequate compensation for cuts and crackles. Another Furtwängler performance (1953), more complete but without Flagstad, comes on HMV RLS 702 and 19-Seraphim 6100; the Rome SO of RAI is less than firstrate, yet Furtwängler moulds a version of conviction and concentration with the assistance of Mödl's Brünnhilde, Frantz's Wotan and outstanding contributions from Frick, Patzak and Greindl. Another veteran performance is Knappertsbusch's of Bayreuth 1957 on Cetra LO 58-61; tempos are deliberate, but the work unfolds mightily, with Hotter a magisterial Wotan, an energetic Brünnhilde from Varnay, a youthful Siegfried in Bernd Aldenhoff.

The Solti *Ring* of 1959-65 on Decca D100D19 and 19-London RING-S made recording history (p. 107) as the first complete studio performance. The Vienna PO under Solti's powerful guidance, Nilsson's brilliant Brünnhilde, the subtle Fricka of Flagstad, and the emphatic Wotan of George London make it still a competitor for the *Ring* prize. Karajan's version was completed in 1972 on Deutsche Grammophon 19-DG 2720051 and has all the chamber subtlety he and the Berlin PO were deploying at the time; Stewart is an imposing

Wotan, Dernesch a Brünnhilde without bombast, Thomas a Siegfried whose panache comes and goes.

A conflation of live Bayreuth performances under Böhm came out in 1973 on Philips 6747037. Böhm's manner with the work is conversational, quick-witted, lean, with the Wotan of Adam and Nilsson's Brünnhilde likewise lessening their lights, though Windgassen's Siegfried is exhilarated by the speed. At the other extreme is *The Ring* in Andrew Porter's English translation (p. 107) with Goodall and the English National Opera in 1978 on HMV SLS 5032, 5063, 875, 5118 and 4-Angel SDC 3825, 5-Angel SX 3826 (first two operas only; *Siegfried* and *Götterdämmerung* are distributed on the Odeon label by Peters International). Tempos are steady to sluggish; yet the thoughtful approach generates a momentum of its own with the fine Brünnhilde of Rita Hunter and the ringing Siegfried of Alberto Remedios.

DIE WALKÜRE

Always the most popular of the *Ring* cycle, *Die Walküre* has many separate recordings. A Furtwängler version with the Vienna PO (1954) on HMV HQM 1019-23 and 5-Seraphim 6012 has compelling lyrical sweep, an exciting Brünnhilde from Mödl, tender yet weighty Wotan from Frantz. Leinsdorf (1962) directs an eloquent performance on Decca 7BB 125-9 and 5-Victor LDS 6706; Nilsson is an athletic Brünnhilde, George London concentrated as Wotan, the ill-starred twins of Brouwenstein and Vickers are intelligently done. *Walküre* highlights appear on The Golden Age of Opera EJS 543 with Leinsdorf directing a 1941 performance including Melchior as commanding Siegmund, Varnay his forceful sister, Traubel an exuberant Brünnhilde, and Schorr a noble Wotan at the end.

Act 2 from 1935 on Seraphim 60190 (from USA) or Electrola IC 049-03023 (from Germany) has loving care from Walter and the Vienna PO and a superlative cast in Lotte Lehmann, Melchior, and Emanuel List. Another magnificent Act 2 (1959) comes on Ace of Diamonds GOS 581-2 and 2-London 1204, with Flagstad, Svanholm, van Mill, and Knappertsbusch powerfully directing the Vienna PO, coupled with the *Götterdämmerung* Dawn, Rhine Journey and Funeral March.   A thrilling *Walküre* Act 1 scene iii with the NBC SO under Toscanini, broadcast in 1941, is sung by Traubel and Melchior on RCA RB 16274 and Victrola VIC LM 2452; the coupling is orchestral excerpts from *Götterdämmerung* (p. 138).

A 1936 Act 2 comes from Education Media Associates on RR 426; Fritz Reiner conducts the incomparable Brünnhilde of Flagstad, Schorr as Wotan, Lotte Lehmann and Melchior as the twins.   Another pre-war Act 2 is equally memorable, with the same twins, Hotter's majestic Wotan, and Bruno Walter lyrically at work with the Vienna PO on HMV DB 3719-28 and Victor M582.   The Todesverkündigung from Act 2 and whole of Act 3 (1958) are on Ace of Diamonds GOS 577-8 and 2-London 1203 in a staggering version from Solti and the Vienna PO, with Flagstad, Svanholm, and Edelmann as a dark and noble Wotan.   Act 1 scene iii and Act 3 are coupled on American CBS 32 26 0018 in a 1945 performance by the New York Philharmonic under Rodzinski; Traubel is imperious Brünnhilde and warm Sieglinde to the Siegmund of Emery Darcy and Janssen's majestic Wotan. A Bayreuth Act 3 under Karajan (1951) on Electrola IC 181-03035/6 has the commanding Brünnhilde of Varnay, a briefly sympathetic Sieglinde in Rysanek, and the finely weighted Wotan of Sigurd Björling.

GÖTTERDÄMMERUNG

A separate *Götterdämmerung* is memorable for Flagstad's Brünnhilde on Decca LXT 5205-10 and 6-London 4603 (1956), though based mainly on Norwegian broadcasts with an orchestra under Fjelstadt inadequate to the task; Svanholm is Siegfried.   Education Media Associates on RR 429 has excerpts with the Covent Garden orchestra under Furtwängler (1937); the star-studded cast includes Flagstad, Melchior, Janssen, Thorborg.   On HMV ALP 1016 and Seraphim 60003 Flagstad sings the Immolation with Furtwängler

132

and the Philharmonia (1954), coupled with a Dawn, Rhine Journey and Funeral March from Furtwängler and the Vienna PO. Highlights from *Götterdämmerung* (1972), sung by a radiant Rita Hunter and full-voiced Remedios are directed by Mackerras with the LPO on Embassy CFP 40008. The end of Act 3, from Siegfried's narration, is performed by the same singers on Unicorn UNS 245-6 (1972), a studio slice of the English *Ring* with Goodall and the ENO at their best.

RING BACKGROUND AND BACKLASH
Invaluable background is provided by Deryck Cooke's perceptive analysis of the motifs on Decca SET 406-8 and 3-London RDN S-1; with it is Solti's *Siegfried Idyll* (p. 142) and the *Kinderkatechismus* (p. 139). Irreverent and hilarious comment from Anna Russell can be savoured on CBS 61665 and 2-Columbia MG 31199.

TRISTAN UND ISOLDE
A much abbreviated Bayreuth version on Electrola IC 181-03 031/3 was conducted by Elmendorff in 1928, with Larsén-Todsen an impressive Isolde, Gunnar Graarud a resounding Tristan, Andresen firm as Marke. A first Karajan set is live from Bayreuth 1952 on Cetra LO 47, intense and powerful; Mödl is a dramatic Isolde, Vinay a Tristan of true nobility, Hotter a moving Kurwenal. The finest performance remains Furtwängler's (1953) with the Philharmonia on HMV RLS 684 and 5-Angel 1508; finest for depth of understanding, Flagstad's towering Isolde, Suthaus as Tristan, Fischer-Dieskau as Kurwenal. The Solti version (1961) on Decca SET 204-8 and 5-London 1502 elicits incandescence from the Vienna PO, splendour from Nilsson's Isolde, commanding performances from Uhl as Tristan, van Mill as Marke. Böhm's 1966 Bayreuth set on Deutsche Grammophon 2740 144 and 5-DG 27 13001 again has an effortless Nilsson, Windgassen's powerful Tristan, a darkly serious Marke from Talvela. Karajan's second version (1973) is on HMV SLS 963 and

5-Angel S-3777; the Berlin PO is incomparable in weight and power, Ridderbusch a regal Marke, Vickers mighty and sometimes magical as Tristan, Dernesch a not quite heroic Isolde.

Tristan excerpts on Great Recordings of the Century HMV and Angel COLH 132, with Leider a direct and forceful Isolde, Melchior a ringing Tristan, span the years 1928-31; the coupling includes 'Ich sah das Kind' from *Parsifal*. A disc from Educational Media Associates has part of a 1936 Covent Garden performance on RR 471; Melchior is again Tristan, List a sympathetic Marke, Flagstad a radiant Isolde. Highlights conducted by Leinsdorf on The Golden Age of Opera EJS 556 include slices from each act on two discs; Melchior is the ubiquitous Tristan, Traubel the generous Isolde, Kipnis a thoughtful Marke. Telefunken DP6.48020 (1952) has Mödl's lyrical and tender Isolde, Windgassen's eloquent Tristan; the Act 1 narration, love duet, and Liebestod are included. Knappertsbusch and the Vienna PO (1960) feature on Decca LXT 5559 and London 25138 with Nilsson, in a no-nonsense Prelude, splendid Act 1 narration, and ravishing Liebestod.

DIE MEISTERSINGER
Nine complete versions may be considered. Furtwängler's Bayreuth performance of 1943 on Electrola IC 181-01 797/801 has some omissions (including the quintet), intensity and pace from the conductor, a vibrant Lorenz as Walther, Prohaska's warm and generous Sachs, a mature Eva in Maria Müller. Karajan at Bayreuth (1951) is on Columbia 33CX 1021-5 and 5-Seraphim IE 6030, impressive and unmannered, with Schwarzkopf a delectable Eva, Edelmann commanding as Sachs, Hopf a firmly lyrical Walther. The moving Knappertsbusch version (1952) on Decca GOM 535-9 enjoys the splendour of the Vienna PO, Gueden as appealing Eva, Treptow an ardent Walther, Schoeffler benign and paternal as Sachs.

Ariola XI 70851R preserves a live Munich performance;

the Bavarian State Opera under Keilberth may be unimaginative, but Claire Watson is a fresh Eva, Thomas a commanding Walther, Hotter a venerable and expressive Sachs. On HMV HQM 1094-8 and 5-Angel 3572 is Kempe's set (1958), lithe without bombast from the Berlin PO, playful in Grümmer's Eva, with Schock an impetuous Walther, Frantz a kindly Sachs. A second Karajan version, with the Dresden State Orchestra (1971) pouring out beautiful sounds on HMV SLS 957 and 5-Angel S-3776, has a notably fresh Eva and Walther in Donath and Kollo, outstanding David in Schreier, contemplative Sachs in Adam.

Varviso's 1974 Bayreuth version is on Philips 6747 167, steadily done, with Bode a girlish Eva, Cox a ringing Walther, Ridderbusch warm as Sachs. Solti's glowing orchestral sound from the Vienna PO (1976) on Decca D13D5 and 5-London 1512 occasionally goes to his head; but Bode and Kollo as Eva and Walther are kittenishly appealing, and Bailey is a sympathetic Sachs. Jochum and the German State Opera, Berlin (1976) are majestic on Deutsche Grammophon 2740 149 and 5-DG 271 3011 with some odd casting; Ligendza overloads Eva, Domingo gets Walther's German wrong, Fischer-Dieskau gets Sachs's too right.

An intelligent and affectionate Act 3 from Böhm and the Dresden Staatskapelle (1938) on Electrola E 80983-4 has Teschemacher a lyrical Eva, Ralf a passionate Walther, Nissen a generous Sachs. On HMV and Angel COLH 137 Schorr sings *Meistersinger* extracts with impeccable diction and rounded tone (1923-43); the quintet includes also Schumann, Parr, Melchior and Ben William. Highlights on The Golden Age of Opera EJS 548 (1928) are sung by the full-voiced Schorr as Sachs, Robert Hull a forthright Walther, Eva Marherr-Wagner a youthful and sensitive Eva.

PARSIFAL
Knappertsbusch conducted the first two complete sets, both from Bayreuth. The 1951 version on Tel-Decca EX 6.35006 has a moving Gurnemanz from Weber, Mödl as

thrilling Kundry, London a powerful Amfortas, Windgassen an eloquent Parsifal. The 1962 performance on Philips 6729 002 and 5-Philips PHS-5-950 has Hotter as magnificent Gurnemanz, Dalis a warmly dramatic Kundry, Thomas a commanding Parsifal, and London's Amfortas yet more doomladen. Boulez's 1970 Bayreuth *Parsifal* is on Deutsche Grammophon 1740 143 and 5-DG 27 13004; tempos are brisk, Jones is a dramatic and telling Kundry, Crass a sympathetic Gurnemanz, King's Parsifal tender and commanding, Stewart a stern Amfortas. Solti's 1973 performance on Decca SET 550-4 and 5-London 1510 stems from the studio and Vienna PO; it has Ludwig as resourceful Kundry, Kollo's authoritative Parsifal, Fischer-Dieskau's nobly intelligent Amfortas, and Frick's gripping Gurnemanz. A very selective issue from Bayreuth 1927 under Karl Muck and Siegfried Wagner was issued on Columbia LCX 36-43 and the orchestral sections under Siegfried Wagner are now available on Electrola IC 147-30647/8 (p. 138).

OUTSTANDING WAGNERIAN SINGERS

The most ambitious celebration of the Bayreuth centenary was a ten-record set, Electrola IC 181 30 669-78; 'Sänger auf dem Grünen Hügel' covers the period 1900-50 with contributions from almost 150 singers, including Lilli Lehmann with 'Du bist der Lenz' (1907), Emmy Destinn in a 1910 Liebestod, Ernest van Dyck with 'Am stillen Herd' (1903). Deutsche Grammophon also produced four fine pairs of discs on DG 2721 109-12, sampling singers from 1900 to 1976. There is some duplication with the Electrola set, the forty singers including sopranos from Destinn to Jones, tenors from Henzel to Thomas, basses from Demuth to Talvela. 'Twenty great Wagnerian singers of the twentieth century' on Rhapsody RHA 6020 adds such remarkable performances as Tauber's Preislied, Melba in 'Sola ne' miei prim' anni' (apparently from *Lohengrin*), and a Liebestod from Nordica. 'Unforgettable voices sing German opera' on RCA VIC 1455 ranges 1929-40, includes Traubel in some

Lohengrin, Rethberg in *Der fliegende Höllander*, Schumann-Heink in Waltraute's narration, and a Flagstad Liebestod of 1935.

The supreme Wagnerians are worth further exploration. Flagstad, for instance, does a magnificent 1937 Immolation on RCA VIC 1517; the disc includes her also in some *Tannhäuser*, *Lohengrin*, and *Walküre*. A record called 'Kirsten Flagstad—In memoriam' (1963), Decca SXL 6042 and London 25778, contains glorious extracts from her complete *Rheingold*, *Walküre* Acts 1 and 3, and two of the Wesendonck songs. Flagstad and Melchior (1939 and 1940) sing *Parsifal* and *Götterdämmerung* duets on RCA RB 6604 and LM 2763. Leider, Melchior and Schorr combine on HMV and Angel COLH 105 in excerpts from *Walküre* and *Götterdämmerung* (1927-30). Melchior on RCA VIC 1500 sings extracts from most of the Wagner tenor roles, excluding Tristan, but including the last two Wesendonck songs (1938-40). Hotter and Nilsson join for Columbia 33CX 1542 and Seraphim S-60167 in parts of *Der fliegende Holländer* and *Walküre* (1958).

OUTSTANDING WAGNERIAN CONDUCTORS

A companion centenary volume, on Deutsche Grammophon 2721 113, recalls Bayreuth conductors from Knappertsbusch in 1928 to Boulez in 1970; Strauss does a deadpan *Holländer* overture (1931), de Sabata a mightily intense *Tristan* prelude (1939). Conductors worth sampling elsewhere include Beecham (1955) on Philips GBL 5635 and Columbia ML1962, electrifying in the *Dutchman* overture, some *Meistersinger*, *Götterdämmerung*, and *Parsifal*. A Wagnerian of distinction in his early days, Boult directs idiomatically and with eloquence on four discs of preludes, overtures, and 'bleeding chunks' (1972-5), plus the *Faust* overture (p. 141) and *Siegfried Idyll* (p. 142); they are HMV ASD 2812, 2934, 3000, 3071 and Angel S-36871, S-36998, S37090 (the third British disc appears not to have been issued in America). On Unicorn WFS 2-3 comes a series of Furtwängler performances (1938 and 1949) with the Vienna PO and Berlin PO, including a sumptuous *Meistersinger* prelude, thoughtful *Dutchman* overture, and flowing *Siegfried Idyll* (p. 141). Karajan and the Berlin PO (1975-6) are unmistakable for good and ill in two discs of preludes and overtures on HMV ASD 3130 and 3160 and 2-Angel S-3610. Klemperer (1960) conducts the Philharmonia in a similar selection that excludes *Parsifal* but includes the Liebestod and Dance of the apprentices on HMV ASD 2695-6 and 2-Angel 3610B. A Solti disc with the Vienna PO on Decca SET 227 and London 9314 (1962) includes the *Rienzi*, *Dutchman*, and *Tannhäuser* overtures with the Paris Venusberg in vivid and impetuous performance.

Szell and the polished Cleveland Orchestra (1967) on CBS 61263 and 3-Columbia D3M-32317 give panache and splendour to the *Rienzi, Dutchman, Faust* (p. 141) overtures, and the preludes to *Lohengrin* Act 1 and *Meistersinger*. Volume five of the 'Toscanini Treasury of Great Music' is devoted to Wagner and has four discs (1936-52) on RCA VCM 4 (issued in America on separate discs); performances of integrity and fire include the *Lohengrin*, *Tristan* and *Meistersinger* preludes, the *Faust* overture (p. 141), *Siegfried Idyll* (p. 141), and excerpts from *The Ring*. A masterful Toscanini Dawn and Rhine journey with the NBC SO comes on RCA RB 16274 and Victrola VIC LM 2452 coupled to *Die Walküre* Act 1 scene iii (p. 132). Siegfried Wagner directs elderly performances of the *Lohengrin* Act 1 and *Tristan* preludes, *Parsifal* excerpts (p. 136), the *Huldigungsmarsch* (p. 142), *Siegfried Idyll* (p. 141), and his own overture to *Der Bärenhäuter* on Electrola IC 147-30647/8. Two discs of the Columbia SO under Bruno Walter (1963) on CBS 78252 and Columbia MS-6149, Odyssey Y-30667 combine the *Siegfried Idyll* (p. 141) with beautifully textured preludes, overtures, Venusberg and Good Friday musics.

Vocal

CHORAL WORKS

Das Liebesmahl der Apostel on Symphonica SYM 11 and Peters PLE 043 has the Ambrosian male-voice choir and Symphonica of London under Wyn Morris in a spacious and well sung performance; the coupling is Bruckner's *Helgoland*. A second version on CBS 76721 and M35131 from Boulez, the Westminster choir, and New York PO is more brusque but also intense; the *Siegfried Idyll* (p. 142) completes the disc.

The *Kinderkatechismus zu Kosels Geburtstag*, in the 1874 version with small orchestra, is performed by the Wiener Sängerknaben and members of the Vienna PO under Solti on Decca SET 406-8 and 3-London RDN S-1 (p. 133).

EARLY SONGS AND ARIA

The Seven compositions for Goethe's *Faust*, with *Der Tannenbaum* and the seven Paris songs are effectively performed by Genadi, Maus, Lang to Gundlich's piano accompaniment on Mixtur MXT 3004. *Der Tannenbaum* and three of the Paris songs in German appear also in a recital by Kónya with Guth as pianist; the disc, MUCS 116, includes songs by Verdi. Elisabeth Schumann sings with orchestra (1938) a German version of *Dors, mon enfant* on the privately recorded set W 301 A-F; the discs include also Lorri Lail and Gerald Moore (1947) in three of the Paris songs and *Der Tannenbaum*; on the same set comes the tenor aria extension Wagner wrote for insertion in Marschner's *Der Vampyr* from Dowd and orchestra under Würmser (1963); the coupling is completed with the *König Enzio* overture (p. 140) and extracts from *Die Hochzeit* and *Das Liebesverbot* (p. 126).

WESENDONCK SONGS

Notable versions with the original piano accompaniment are Flagstad and Moore on HMV DB 6841-2, DB 6749, a memorable partnership; Lotte Lehmann in nos. 3 and 5 with

Ulanowsky on American Columbia 71496D.

The Mottl orchestral version (Wagner orchestrated only *Träume*) has been often recorded. Flagstad's performance of 1956 on Decca SDD 212 and London 25101 takes pride of place; it is radiant and relaxed, with Knappertsbusch and the Vienna PO; she sings also extracts from *Lohengrin*, *Walküre*, *Parsifal*. Janet Baker does them sensuously and expressively with the LPO and Boult on HMV ASD 3260 and Angel S-37199 (1976); coupling is the Brahms *Alto Rhapsody* and Strauss songs. Horne couples the songs with the Mahler *Kindertotenlieder* on Decca SXL 6466 and London 26147 (1970); the accompaniment with the RPO under Henry Lewis is poised and assured. Kniplová with the Czech PO under Košler gives a radiant performance on Supraphon MS 1136 (1972); the coupling is an unsmiling *Siegfried Idyll*. Moreira on Turnabout TV 34281S and Vox 12320 (1964) sings tenderly with the Innsbruck SO under Robert Wagner; also included are the *Alto Rhapsody*, Mahler Rückert songs, and Schumann *Requiem for Mignon*. Nilsson is rapt and remote in a coupling that includes arias from *Die Feen*, *Rienzi*, *Der fliegende Holländer* on Philips 6500 294 (1972); the accompaniment by the LSO and Colin Davis is careful and passionate. Again with Davis and the LSO, Jessye Norman on Philips 9500 031 (1976) maintains a lyrical and warm line; the *Tristan* Prelude and Liebestod make up the disc.

Orchestral music

EARLY OVERTURES AND SYMPHONY

The overture to *König Enzio* appears on the privately recorded W 301 A-F under Leo Würmser in a coupling with songs, an aria, and operatic excerpts (p. 126). The *Columbus* overture can be heard under Richard Kraus on the privately recorded Penzance 8. The *Polonia* overture on Urania 57116 is played by the Leipzig Radio Orchestra under Pflüger, in an alert coupling with the Symphony under Guhl and the Berlin Radio SO. The version of the Symphony by the Bamberg SO under Gerdes (1972) on Deutsche Grammophon DG 2530 194, coupled with the *Rienzi* and *Faust* overtures, is less subtle and sometimes slipshod.

FAUST, TRAUERMUSIK, TRÄUME

Acceptable versions of the *Faust* overture are those of Toscanini (1946), cleanly limned in the set on RCA VCM 4 and LM 7032 (p. 138); George Szell with the beautiful sheen of the Cleveland Orchestra on CBS 6063 and 3-Columbia D3M-32317 (1967); Boult eloquent but undramatic with the LPO (1975) on HMV ASD 3071 and S-37090 (p. 137).

The *Trauermusik* on themes from *Euryanthe*, composed for Weber's reburial in Dresden, can be heard in a coupling with the *Huldigungsmarsch* and some Mendelssohn, competently performed by the band of the Paris Police under Dondeyne on Westminster WMS-1008 (1954).

Träume, the last of the Wesendonck songs, was arranged by Wagner for violin and small orchestra; it is played by Hugh Bean and the Philharmonia under Kletzki on HMV ALP 1696 and Angel S-35765 (1959) with the *Siegfried Idyll* and Brahms-Haydn Variations.

SIEGFRIED IDYLL

Among innumerable performances may be selected Siegfried Wagner, who inspired and heard the first performance (unless he was asleep), on Electrola IC 147-30647/8 with more of his father's music (pp. 136, 138) and some of his own; Toscanini (1936) on the RCA VCM 4 set and LVT 1004 (p. 138); Furtwängler and the VPO in a warm and flowing version (1949) on Unicorn WFS 2-3, coupled with other Wagner (p. 137); Bruno Walter and the Columbia SO on CBS 78252 and Columbia MS-6149 (1963), gentle and lovingly turned; Barenboim and the ECO (1968) on HMV ASD 2346 and Angel S-36484, expressive, a bit weighty, coupled with Schoenberg's *Verklärte Nacht* and Hindemith's *Trauermusik*; Marriner and the Academy of St. Martin-in-the-Fields on Argo ZRG 604 (1969), with unfailing distinction of sound, coupled with the now rejected Adagio for clarinet and strings and Strauss's *Metamorphosen*; Solti with members of the Vienna PO (1969) in a sensitive and delicious chamber performance on Decca SET 406-8 and 3-London RDN S-1 (p. 133) and as filler to Bruckner Symphony no 7 on Decca SET 324 and 2-London 2216; a cool and generously-shaped version from Boult and the LSO (1974) on HMV ASD 3000, coupled with the *Parsifal* prelude and other extracts; Karajan and the Berlin PO, as fill-up to Bruckner Symphony no 7 (1977) on Deutsche Grammophon 2707 102 and 2-DG 2702 102, lovely but almost too rounded; Boulez and the New York PO (1979) on CBS 76721 and M35131, unleisured but well turned in chamber proportions, coupled with the *Liebesmahl* (p. 139).

MARCHES
The three late Marches, *Huldigungsmarsch* (in full orchestral dress by Wagner and Raff), *Kaisermarsch*, and *American Centennial March*, are played by the LSO under Janowski (1973) on HMV ASD 2837 and Angel S-36879 with due sonority and coupled with vital versions of the *Feen* and *Liebesverbot* overtures. Siegfried Wagner conducts the *Huldigungsmarsch* with the LSO on Electrola IC 147-30647/8, a recording more interesting for its associations than sound, but including more orchestral Wagner (pp. 136, 138).

Piano music

ORIGINAL WORKS
A selection including the A major (plus intrusive fugue) and Wesendonck sonatas, Fantasia, album leaves for the Princess and Betty Schott, is poetically played by Werner Genuit (1973) on Acanta EB 23.049, coupled with a Bülow ballade and four Liszt pieces; the two discs are entitled 'Klaviermusik im Hause Wagner'. The complete piano works, with the exception of the Wesendonck polka and Ernst Kietz's Song without words, are deftly done by Martin Galling (1963)

142

on 2-Turnabout TV 34654-5S; some of the versions need updating.

LISZT ARRANGEMENTS AND JEUX D'ESPRIT

David Wilde gives a superb performance on Saga 5437 (1976) of Liszt operatic paraphrases: the disc includes the *Dutchman* spinning chorus and Senta's ballad, Elsa's bridal procession (*Lohengrin*), and the Liebestod; there are also reminiscences of *Lucia di Lammermoor* and *Norma*.

Fauré, Messager, and Chabrier expressed their irreverent devotion to Wagner in piano duet quadrilles on his themes. *Souvenirs de Bayreuth* (on *Ring* motifs) by Fauré and Messager, and Chabrier's *Souvenir de Munich* (based on *Tristan*) are coupled with other duets in sparkling performances by Kyriakou and Klien on Turnabout TV 34234S.

Index

Note: b before a page number refers to a book, e to an edition, r to a recording; artists in the selected recordings are not indexed

Abraham, G b 101, e 125
Aeschylus 9, 22, 58, 70, 89, 97-8
Agoult, Comtesse Marie d' 35, 36, 58, 60, 65
Almeida, A de e 115
Altmann, W b 81
America 65, 67, 70, 101
American Centennial March, see *Grosser Festmarsch*
Ander, A 41
Anders, G E 18
Anderson, G F 32
Apel, T 14, 15, 17
Appia, A b 107
Aristophanes 22, 58
Art and revolution 25, 77
Artwork of the future, The 25, 77, 78
Auber, D F 14, 18, 37, 39, 77, e 125
Augusta, Princes of Prussia 39
Avenarius, Cäcilie see Geyer, C
Avenarius, E 17, 20, 56, 83

Bach, J S 12, 13, 69
Baermann, H J e 112, r 142
Bailey, R W 89, b 102
Bakunin, M 23, 24
Balling, M e 110-12, 113, 121
Barker, F G b 102
Barth, H b 80, b 88
Barzun, J b 98-9
Baudelaire, C P 38, b 86
Bayreuth 14, 16, 18, 50, 57 58, 59, 61, 64, 79, 81, 86, 92, 96, 100, 108, 109, 110, 116, 125, 143; Bibiena theatre 57, 59, 61, 108; centenary 89, 101, r 136, r 137; festival 59, 62, 65-6, 68, 84, b 85, 86, b 87-8, 89, 93, b 107-8, 108, 116; finances 61, 62, 63, 65, 66, 67; recordings 127-8, 129, 130, 131, 132, 133, 134, 135-6, 137; Richard Wagner Archive 112; Richard 59, 61, 64, 77, 79, 92, 127; W's letters from b 83; W's residence in 59-74 (see also Wahnfried); Youth festival r 126-7
Bayreuther Blätter 68, 73, 77, 83
Beethoven, L van 9, 19, 22, 57, 58, 61, 69; Ninth Symphony 12, 18, 22, 23, 25, 60, 108; other works 11, 12, 26, 31, 40, 63
Beethoven (Wagner) 58, 77, 78, 91
Bekker, P b 94
Bellini, V 13, 14, 61, 72, 78, 111, 143
Bennett, J b 87-8, 94
Berlin 15, 19, 20, 22, 43, 44, 59, 61, 63, 65, 71-2, 81, 115; Royal Academy of Arts 55, 59
Berlioz, H 19, 33, 35, 37, 38, 40, 55
Bethmann, H 14
Betz, F 64
Bianchi, E e 121
Biebrich 42
Bischoff, Professor 25
Bismarck, O von 29, 59, 71, 99
Bissing, H von 44
Bizet, G 64
Blassmann, A e 124
Boieldieu, F 69
Boito, A 31, 120, 121
Boucher, M b 99
Brahms, J 43, 62, 63, 64, r 140, r 141

145

Brandt, C W's letters to 83
Brecher, G e 119
Breig, W e 114
Brissler, F e 120
Brink, L b 104
Brockhaus, Friedrich 12
Brockhaus, Heinrich 24
Brockhaus, Luise see Wagner, L
Bruckner, A 53, 61-2, r 139, r 142
Brussels 38, 121
Buesst, A b 104
Bülow, Blandine von 43, 46, 50
Bülow, Daniela von 46, 50, 84
Bülow, Hans von 27, 34, 35, 36,
    37, 39, 42, 43, 46, 47, 50,
    52, 54, 55, 57, 60, e 120,
    e 121, e 124, e 125, r 142;
    and Bayreuth 62; as conductor
    27, 48, 52, 53, 55; letters of
    b 84
Bulwer Lytton, E G 16, 17, 102
Burbidge, P b 89
Burk, J N b 81
Burlingame, E L b 78, 80
Burrell Collection b 81, 82, 83,
    90, 97
Burrell, Hon M 81, b 90, 95
Busoni, F e 124
Butler, P b 107
Byron, Lord G 11, 26

Calderón de la Barca, P 35
Cantor, C b 106
Capitulation, A 58, 77
Cesardi, T O e 120
Chabrier, E e 124, r 143
Chamberlain, H S 82, b 93, 95,
    b 101
Chancellor, J b 97
Chiswick District Library 126
Chorley, H 94
Cleather, A b 100
Cobden, R 38
Communication to my friends, A
    28, 77, 80
Constantine, Prince of Sachsen-
    Weimar 10
Cooke, D 89, b 103, e 117, r 133
Cornelius, P 41, 42-3, 45, 46,
    47, 51, 53-4, 61, 63

Crockow, Count 60
Crump, B b 100
Culshaw, J b 107

Dahlhaus, C b 101, e 112-14
Dangl, Frau 47
Dannreuther, E 67, b 76, b 78,
    b 87
Dante Alighieri 9, 11, 32, 106
Darwin, C 69, 98-9
Daube, O e 123
Davison, H b 87
Davison, J W b 87
Deathridge, J b 102
Debussy, C b 106
Dent, E J 119
Dickinson, A E F b 105
Dietsch, P L 39
DiGaetani, J L b 98, b 103
Dittmar, Dean 60
Doepler, C E 65, b 85
Donington, R b 103
Donizetti, G 18, e 125, 143
Doré, G 38
Dorn, H 16, 31, 108
Dresden 25, 26, 27, 28, 29,
    34, 37, 42, 43, 48, 51, 60,
    69, 83, 108, 111, 112, 115,
    119, 120, 141; court theatre
    19, 21, 22, 47, 78, 112, 119;
    revolution 23-4, 39, 47, 88;
    Vaterlandsverein 23, 77, 79;
    W's letters to Dresden friends
    b 82; W's residence in 19-24
Düfflipp, L von 56
Du Moulin Eckart, R b 84, b 108
Dvořák, A 43
Dyck, G van den e 121

Ebers, G M 59
Egypt, Khedive of 62
Ellis, W A 23, 76, b 77-8, 79,
    80, 83, 85, 88, b 90
Erard, Mme 35
Euripides 11, 22
Evans, E senior b 78

Fauré, G e 125, r 143
Faust overture 18, 32, e 111, e
    123, e 124, r 137, r 138, r 141

146

Feen, Die 13, 73, e 110-11,
e 115, e 120, r 126-7, r 140,
r 142; in Munich 110-11
Feustel, F 65, 71; W's letters to
b 83
Finck, H T 91, b 93, e 121
Fischer, W W's letters to b 82
Fischer-Dieskau, D b 98
Fladt, H e 114
Fliegende Holländer, Der 19, 60,
77, 80, 88, b 92, b 102, b 107,
e 115, e 116, e 118, e 119,
e 120, e 124, r 127-8, r 137,
r 138, r 140, r 143; con-
ception of 16; composition
of 18, 37; in Dresden 20; in
Zürich 25, 30, 32; in Munich
47, 70; in Mannheim 61; in
Budapest 63; in London 76;
in Bologna 77
Florence 55, 66
Förster, Bernhard 70
Franco-Prussian war 57-8, 61, 62
Frederick the Great 45
Friedrich Augustus I of Saxony
111
Friedrich Augustus II of Saxony
20, 23, 111, 122
Friedrich Barbarossa 23

Gade, N 22
Gal, H b 96
Garibaldi, G 33, 39
Garten, H F b 99
Gatty, C T b 106
Gautier (Mendès), J 9, 55, 66, 68,
72, b 85-6, 121
Geck, M e 112, e 114
German art and German politics
52, 77
Geyer (Avenarius), Cäcilie 10,
17, 20, 55-6, 83
Geyer, L H C 9, 10, 11, 56, 61,
97
Gilman, L b 101
Glasenapp, C F b 90, 92, 93, 95
Gluck, C W 13, 22, 44, 61, e 125
Glückliche Bärenfamilie, Die 15
Gobineau, Comte J A de 71, 72,
74

Goethe, J W von 9, 10, 22, 26
35, 42, 69, 104, 111, 121, 139
Goldman, A b 79
Goldwag, B 67; W's letters to b 82
Gollancz, V b 108
Golther, W e 121
Götterdämmerung 63, 74, 100,
b 102, e 118, e 124, r 131,
r 132-3, r 137, r 138; con-
ception of 23 (see also *Sieg-
frieds Tod*); composition of
56, 60, 63, 66; in Bayreuth
65-6; in London 76; see also
Ring des Nibelungen, Der
Gotthelf, F e 123
Gounod, C 37, 38, 60
Gozzi, C 11, 13
Graves, M H b 98
Gregor-Dellin, M b 80-81, b 84
Grosser Festmarsch 65, e 111,
e 123, r 142
Gutman, R W b 96

Habeneck, F A 18
Hadden, J C b 100-101
Hadow, W H b 93, b 95-6
Halévy, J F e 125
Hamburg 62
Hanslick, E 41, 43, b 87, 91
Harewood, Earl of b 100
Hatzfeld-Wildenburg, Paul Graf
von 38
Haussmann, G E 37
Heckel, E 62; W's letters to b 83
Heine, F W's letters to b 82
Helena Pavlovna, Grand Duchess
44
Helmholtz, H 61, 63
Henderson, W J b 93
Herodom and Christendom 72, 78
Herwegh, Emma 29, 42
Herwegh, George 29, 31
Hight, G A b 95
Hiller F 22, 87
Hime, Major H W L b 88
Hindemith, P r 141
Hitler, A 89, 96, 99, 109, 112
Hochkofler, M e 116, e 117
Hochzeit, Die 13, e 110, 115,
r 126, 139

Hoffmann E T A 10
Hohe Braut, Die 15
Hohenlohe-Schillingsfürst, Prince
    Chlodwig 51
Holtei, K von 111
Homer 9, 11, 45, 55
Hopkinson, C b 102
Hueffer, F b 82, b 87, 88, b 106,
    122
Hugo, V 48-9, 58
Huldigungsmarsch 46, 47, e 111,
    e 123, e 124, r 138, r 141, r 142
Humperdinck, E 73, 74, e 118,
    e 124
Hurn, P D 91, b 97
Hussey, D e 117, e 123
Hutcheson, E b 104

Irvine, D b 80, b 93, b 104,
    b 106

Jachmann, H b 108
Jacob, G e 117, e 123
Jacobs, R L b 96
Jesus von Nazareth 24, 78, 104
Jewishness in music 27, 54, 55,
    77, 79, 96
John, king of Saxony 39
Johnson, T A e 123
Jones, K V e 125
Jullien, A b 86, 93
June, F e 121
Junge Siegfried, Der 28, 29, 30

Kaisermarsch 58, 61, e 111,
    e 123, e 124, r 142
Kalergis (Muchanoff), M 38, 43
Kapp, J b 94
Karlsruhe 40, 44, 45, 60, 61
Keller, R e 120
Keppler, Dr 75
Kerman, J b 105
Kietz, E B 19, 27, 113, 123, 142
Kinderkatechismus 62, 63, e 115,
    e 121, 133, r 139
Kleinmichel, R e 118, e 119,
    e 121
Klink, C G 112, e 120, e 121
Klindworth K e 118, e 119, e 121
Kniese, J 114, e 115-16

Know thyself 71, 78
Kobbé, G b 92-3, b 100
Koenig, R b 107-8
Kogel, G F e 118, e 119
Königsberg 15, 19
Krehbiel, H 93, b 100
Kunstwerk der Zukunft, Der see
    Artwork of the future, The

Large, B b 107
Laube, H 13, 15, 20, 53, 80
Laussot family 26
Laussot, Jessie (Taylor and Hille-
    brand) 26, 53, 55, 66
Lavignac, A b 100
Lehmann, L 64, b 86, r 136
Lehrs, S 19, 59
Leibnitz, G W 52
Leipzig 9, 11, 12, 13, 15, 18, 19,
    43, 54, 64, 71, 115; battle of
    9, 71; St Nicholas's school 11;
    St Thomas's school 12; univ-
    ersity 12, 28
Lenrow, E b 83
Lepsius, K R 61
Leroy, L A b 104
Lesimple, A b 86
Leubald und Adelaide 11
Levi, H 72, 111, e 120
Levy, O b 84
Lewald, A e 122
Lidgey, C A b 93
Liebesmahl der Apostel, Das
    20-21, e 111, e 121, r 139,
    r 142
Liebesverbot, Das 14, 15, 17,
    e 111, e 115, e 118, 126,
    r 127, 139, r 142
Liepe, E e 121
Lipinski, K 21
Lippert, W b 94
Liszt (Ollivier), Blandine 31, 38,
    40, 41, 43
Liszt, Cosima see Wagner,
    Cosima
Liszt, Franz 19, 24, 25, 26, 27,
    28, 30, 31, 33, 34, 35, 37,
    39, 40, 41, 46, 48, 52, 53,
    56, 57, 60, 61, 63, 67, 68,
    69, 72, b 95, r 142; as

conductor 24, 26, 31, 41, 61;
as pianist 19, 34, 53, 63, 64,
69, 74; and the Cosima/W
relationship 52, 54, 57, 60;
correspondence with W 28,
30, 32, 76, b 82, 103; W arrangements by e 124, r 143
Lohengrin 26, 28, 38, 40, 45,
49, e 110, e 115, e 117,
e 118-19, e 120, e 124, r 129-30
r 136, r 137, r 138, r 140,
r 143; conception of and text
19, 21, 22; composition of
22; in Weimar 26, 48; in
Zürich 30; in Munich 40, 46,
51-2, 70; in Vienna 40, 64,
65; in New York 76; in
Bologna 77
London 12, 16-17, 32-3, 58, 65,
67, 73, 76, 85, 88, 93, 95,
107, 126
Lorenz, A 101
Louis XIV of France 52, 55
Lucerne 9, 27, 37, 50 (see also
Tribschen)
Ludwig II of Bavaria 9, 40, 45,
46, 47, 48, 49, 52, 53, 55-6,
57, 58, 64, 65, 74, 75, 77,
80, 93, 103, 106, 112; rescues
W 45-6; banishes W 49; and
the Bülow/W scandal 50-51,
54; plans to abdicate 50;
engagement to Princess
Sophie 51, 52; anger with W
52, 56; and Bayreuth 58, 60,
62, 66, 70; last meeting with
W 70
Luthers Hochzeit 54
Lüttichau, W A A von 19, 21,
22, 24

Macfarren, N e 119, e 120
Mack, D b 80, b 84, b 88
Magdeburg 14, 54, 111
Magee, B b 99
Mahler, G r 140
Maier, M 42, 44, 46, 47, 53,
66, 67
Mainz 41, 42, 115
Mander, R b 89

Mann, T b 98, b 103, 105
Mannheim 61, 62, 83
Marienbad 21
Marschner, H A 13, e 111, r 126,
r 139
Marx K 23, 66, 98-9
Materna, A 63
Mayer, H b 89
Mein Leben 10, 14, 34, 49, 54,
57, 65, 70, 80-81, 90, 91, 92,
94, 95; dictation of 48, 50,
54, 80
Meistersinger von Nürnberg, Die
40, 43, 46, 50, 51, 52, 62,
65, 101, b 105-6, e 114,
115, e 117, e 118, e 119,
e 121, e 124, e 125, r 134-5,
r 136, r 137, r 138; con-
ception and text 21, 41, 42,
43; composition of 41, 42,
43, 44, 50, 51, 52; in Munich
53; in Vienna 57
Mendelssohn-Bartholdy, F 15,
27, 32, 74, 87, r 141
Mendès, C 9
Meser, C F 21, 115
Messager, A e 125, r 143
Metternich-Sándor, Princess
Pauline 38, 40, 41, 114, 123,
142
Meyer, F 42, 43, 44
Meyerbeer, G 13, 16, 17, 18, 19,
25, 26, 27, 31, 33, 37, 39,
40, 61, 108
Meysenbug, M von 33, 38, 53,
57, 66, 68, b 85; W's
letters to 55, b 83
Michotte, E b 86
Millington, B 89
Mines of Falun, The 19
Mitchinson, J b 89
Moltke, H Graf von 61
Montez, L 49
Moscow 9, 43
Mosley, O b 98
Mottl, F e 115-16, e 117, e 118,
e 119, e 122, e 124, r 140
Mozart, W A 14, 45, 51, 61,
75, 86
Müller, A 25

149

Muncker, T W's letters to 83
Munich 37, 45, 50, 51, 52, 53,
    55, 56, 58, 60, 66, 70, 72, 82,
    93, 111, 124, 134, 143; W's
    residence in 47-9
Music of the future 78
My life see *Mein Leben*

Napoleon Bonaparte 9, 52
Napoleon III of France 38, 39,
    58
Neumann, A 45, 57, 64, 71, 72,
    74, b 85
Newman, E 29, 76, 80, 85.
    b 90-92, 93, 95, 96, 97, 118,
    122
*Nibelungen myth as sketch for a
    drama, The* 78
Niemann, A 36, 39, 40, 71
Nietzsche (Förster), E b 81-2
Nietzsche, F 10, 42, 68, 70,
    77, 92, b 98, 105; meets W
    54; visits Tribschen 55, 56,
    59; in Bayreuth 60, 63, 66;
    last meeting with W 66;
    correspondence with W b
    81-2; *The birth of tragedy* 59,
    77, b 84; *Richard Wagner in
    Bayreuth* 66, b 84; *Human
    all-too-human* 68, b 84; *The
    case of Wagner* b 84; *Nietzsche
    contra Wagner* b 84; *Selected
    aphorisms* b 84; *Ecce homo*
    b 84-5
Nuitter (pseudonym of Truinet),
    C 116, 117, 120
Nuremberg 14, 41, 50, 100

Oedipus 104
Offenbach, J 58
On conducting 77, 78
On German opera 13, 78
On state and religion 77
Opera and drama 28, 46, 77,
    78, 101
Osborne, C b 79, b 89

Pachta, J 12
Padmore, E b 96-7
Page, C b 109

Palermo 72-3
Palestrina, G P da e 125
Panofsky, W b 88-9
Paris 9, 12, 16, 17, 20, 22, 25,
    26, 27, 31, 35, 41, 48, 57,
    58, 68, 76, 80, 85; W's
    residences in 17-19, 37-40;
    songs composed in 17, e 111,
    e 113, e 121, e 122, r 139;
    Tannhäuser in 24, 38-40, 86;
    W's writings in 18, 78, 79
Parsifal (originally *Parzival*)
    14, 21, 66, 67, 70, b 92, 95,
    99, 100, 101, b 106, e 112-13,
    e 114, 115, e 118, e 119,
    e 121, e 124, e 125, r 134,
    r 135-6, r 137, r 138, r 140,
    r 142; conception and text 34,
    49, 56, 67, 68, 86, 114;
    composition of 65, 66-70,
    72-3; projected Munich per-
    formance 68; Bayreuth pro-
    duction 70, 72, 73-4, 77,
    92, 107, 114
Pätz, Johanna (W's mother)
    see Wagner, Johanna
Pauder, O von e 125
Paul, Prince of Thurn and Taxis
    49, 51
Pecht, F 18, 22, 47
Pedro II, Dom, emperor of
    Brazil 34, 66
Pfistermeister, F S von 45, 47,
    48
Pfordten, L von der 47, 49
Pilgrimage to Beethoven, A 18, 78
Pittman, J e 120
Planer, Minna see Wagner, Minna
Planer (Bilz) Natalie 14, 25, 81
Plato 31
Pleasants, H III b 87
Plutarch 11
Porges, H 46, 114
Porter, A 104, b 107, 131
Pourtalès, Countess 40, 41, 42,
    114, 123
Pourtalès, G de b 94-5
Praeger, F b 85, 90, 91, 96
Praetorius, E e 123
Prague 43, 44

Pringle, C 74
Proudhon P J 25
Pusinelli, A 21, 37, 42, 48, 50,
  W's letters to b 83

Raff, J e 123, e 124, r 142
Randegger, A e 122
Raphael, R b 99
Rastrelli, J 20
Rayner, R M b 106
Reissiger, G 20
Religion and art 70, 78
Renoir, A 73
Reutter, I von 51
Rheingold, Das 37, 38, 75, 105,
  e 118, e 124, r 137; con-
  ception and text 29, 30;
  composition of 31; in Munich
  55, 56; in Bayreuth 65, 66;
  see also *Ring des Nibelungen,*
  Der
Richter, H 51, 57, 58, 63, 64,
  65, 71, 110; as conductor
  of W's works 55, 56, 63, 65, 67
Rienzi 17, 22, 25, 82, 101,
  b 102, e 112, e 114, e 115-16,
  e 118-19, e 120, e 124, r 127,
  r 138, r 140, r 141; conception
  of 16; composition of 16, 18;
  in Dresden 19-20; in Zürich
  30; in London 76
Riga 15, 16, 31
Rigolboche, Mme 52
Rimsky-Korsakov, N 87
Ring des Nibelungen, Der 32,
  33, 34, 43, 47, 59, 60, 61,
  71, 74, 76, 85, 94, 95, 97,
  100, 101, b 102-5, r 104, r
  107, e 114, 115, e 117-19,
  e 121, e 124, e 125, r 130-33,
  r 138, 143; conception
  and text 23, 28-9, 30, 31,
  43, 44, 46, 61, 80, 100, 104,
  b 107; composition of 31,
  46; in Bayreuth 53, 62-3,
  64-6, 73, 77, 85, 87-8, 93,
  b 108; in Leipzig 71; in Berlin
  71-2; in London 72; in Russia
  72; see also *Götterdäm-*
  merung, Junge Siegfried,

Rheingold, Siegfried, Sieg-
  frieds Tod, Walküre
Ritter, Alexander 83
Ritter, Julie 26, 27
Ritter, Karl 27, 36
Röckel, A 22, 23, 51, 53, 78,
  e 119, e 120; W's letters to
  51, b 82, 103
Röckl, S b 103
Rome 21, 48, 53, 66
Root W L 91, b 97
Rossini, G 31, 38, 68, 73, 77, 86
Rubinstein, A 43, 63
Rubinstein, J 59, 73, e 116, e
  119, e 120, e 121, e 124
Runciman, J F b 95
Ruskin, J 87

Saint-Saëns, C 38, 53
St Petersburg 43, 44
Sand, G 45
Sarazenin, Die (*Saracen woman,*
  The) 19, 78
Schiller, J C F von 11, b 98
Schittenhelm, A 114
Schleinitz, Countess M 59
Schlesinger, M 18, e 122, e 125
Schnorr von Carolsfeld, J 22
Schnorr von Carolsfeld, Ludwig
  48, 53, 77
Schnorr von Carolsfeld, Malvina
  48, 51
Schoenberg, A r 141
Schopenhauer, A 29, 31, 32, 33,
  54, 58, 95, 101
Schott, Betty 114, 124, 142
Schott, Franz 41, 42, 43, 62
Schott's Söhne (publishers) 12,
  38, 47, 115
Schröder-Devrient, W 12, 13, 15,
  16, 17, 20, 21, 75
Schuler, J b 104
Schumann, Clara 88
Schumann, Robert 17, 19, 22,
  64, r 140
Schwabe, Mme 38, 48
Scott, W 45
Scribe, E 15, 16, 18
Seebach, A L von 39, 40
Seidl, A 74, 112, 122

Semper, G 22, 24, 47
Serov, A 43, 56
Shakespeare, W 9, 11, 14, 16,
    17, 45, 46, 49, 54, 70, 73, 74
Shall we hope? 78
Shaw, G B 67, 76, 85, b 88, 89,
    98, b 102-3, 104
Sieger, Die 33, 53, 68
Siegfried 35, 55, e 118, e 124,
    e 125, r 131; composition of
    (see also *Junge Siegfried*) 34,
    46, 54, 56, 58; in Munich
    58; in Bayreuth 65-6; see also
    Ring des Nibelungen, Der
Siegfried Idyll 46, 58, e 111,
    e 115, e 123, e 124, 125,
    r 133, r 137, r 138, r 139,
    r 140, r 141-2
Siegfrieds Tod 23, 25, 27, 28,
    30, b 102, 103; see also
    Götterdämmerung
Siena 70, 73
Singer, O e 118, e 119, e 121
Skelton, G b 79, b 84, b 108,
    b 109
Slonimsky, N b 86-7
Sokoloff, A H b 108-9
Sonneck, O G b 97
Sophie, Duchess in Bavaria 51
Sorrento 66
Spohr, L 77
Spontini, G 18, 77
Sprinchorn, E b 79
Stein, Jack M b 101
Stein, Leo b 99
Sternfeld, R e 117
Strauss, R 87, r 137, r 140,
    r 142
Strobel, G b 81
Strohm, R e 112, e 114
Strunk, O b 78, 102
Sullivan, Sir A e 120
Sutton, R b 89
Symphony in C 12, 74, e 112,
    e 113, e 122-3, r 140-41

Tanner, M 89
Tannhäuser 22, 24, 32, 33, 40,
    77, 87, 100, b 102, e 102,
    108, e 110, 115, e 116-17,
e 118, e 119, e 120, e 124,
    r 128-9, r 137, r 138; con-
    ception of 19; composition of
    21, 39; in Dresden 21; in
    Weimar 24; in Zürich 30, 32; in
    Paris 38, 39, 40, 79, b 86; in
    Munich 52; in Karlsruhe 61;
    in Vienna 64
Tausig, K 36, 42-3, 59, e 121,
    e 124
Taylor, R b 97
Tchaikovsky, P 87
Terry, E M b 89
Thompson, H b 105-6
Thum, Professor 24
Tichatschek, J 20, 24, 36, 51
Tolstoy, Count L 87
Tours, B e 120
Tribschen 37, 71, 84, 85; W's
    residence in 50-59
Tristan und Isolde 31, 38-9,
    40, 54, 71, 82, 84, 85, 100,
    101, b 105, e 110, e 114, 115,
    e 117, e 118, e 119, e 120-21,
    e 124, e 125, r 133-4, r 136,
    r 137, r 138, r 140, r 143;
    conception and text 32, 33,
    34, 35; composition of 34,
    35, 36, 37; in Vienna 40, 41,
    45; in Munich 47, 48, 55,
    70; in Berlin 65
Turgeniev, I S 44
Turing, P b 108
Turkey, Sultan of 62
Turner, W J 91, b 95

Uhlig, T 26, 27, 28, 30, 32,
    e 118, e 119, e 120; W's
    letters to b 82, 103

Vaillant, Dr 33
Vauthrot, E e 120
Venice 36-7, 41, 70, 72, 73,
    74-5, 94
Verdi, G 64, r 139
Viardot-Garcia, P 38
Victoria, Queen of England 32,
    67
Victors, The see *Sieger, Die*
Vienna 23, 40, 43, 44, 45, 57,

63, 64, 65, 67, 77, b 87,
107, 110, 116
Villiers de l'Isle Adam, P A 9
Voltaire, F M A de 45
Voss, E b 80, b 88, e 112, e 113,
e 114

Wagenseil, C 105-6
Wagner, Adolf (W's uncle) 11
Wagner, Albert (W's brother) 13,
20, 39
Wagner, Cosima (Liszt, von
Bülow) 14, 15, 34, 36, 44,
46, 47, 49, 50, 53, 54, 59,
60, 61, 62, 64, 65, 66, 70,
71, 73, 74, 75, 79, 80, 81,
84, 90, 93, 94, 97, b 108-9,
115; first meeting with W 31;
as Bülow's wife 34-5, 84;
increasing friendship with W
41, 42, 43, 44, 46, 48; final
decision for W 54; divorce
from Bülow 55, 57; marriage
to W 57; at Tribschen 9, 50,
51, 53, 54, 55, 56, 57, 58; at
Wahnfried 62, 63, 66, 67, 68,
69, 71, 72, 73, 74; and the
1876 festival 65; diaries of
23, 53, 55, 61, 63, 66, 72,
73, 79, 81, b 84, 92, 108; as
festival director 107, 109,
116; editorial policy of 82,
83, e 115-16
Wagner (Chamberlain) Eva
(W's daughter) 54, 71
Wagner family, W's letters to b
83, b 108-9
Wagner, Friedelind (W's
granddaughter) b 109
Wagner, Gottfried (W's great-
grandson) b 89
Wagner, Isolde (W's daughter)
48, 50, 54, 55, 71
Wagner, Johanna (W's niece)
19-20, 24, 30, b 108
Wagner, Johanna (Pätz) (W's
mother) 10, 19, 22, 56
Wagner, (Karl) Friedrich (W's
father) 9, 10

Wagner (Wolfram), Klara (W's
sister) 33, 43
Wagner (Brockhaus), Luise (W's
sister) 58
Wagner, Minna (Christiane
Wilhelmine Planer) (W's first
wife) 20, 23, 24, 26-7, 29,
30, 31, 34, 35, 36, 37, 38,
41, 48, 81, 94, 97; first
meeting with W 14; marriage
to W 15; loyalty to W 17, 19,
25; stormy relationship with
W 15, 16, 26, 28, 33, 35, 42;
last meeting with W 43;
death of 50; W's letters to
15, 40, 81, b 83
Wagner, Richard, ancestry and
paternity 9, 10, 56, 84, 90,
97; appearance 18, 25, 29,
55; character 13, 18, 21, 27,
29, 30, 37, 43, 52, 53, 59,
60, 63, 68, 70, 73, 74, 84,
85, 87; as actor and producer
64, 65, 86; as conductor 13,
14, 27, 29, 67, 74, 85, 86,
87, 96; as editor 53, e 120;
as orchestrator 15, 70, 87; as
revolutionary, 22-4, 78, 82, b 90
works: arrangements, 18,
e 125; journals: annals 29,
51, 52, 92; *Autobiographical
sketch* 20, 53, 77, 78, b 80,
87, 92; Red Book 14, 16, b 79,
80, 92; Brown Book 49, 50,
53, b 79-80, 92; Venice diary
36, b 83; see also *Mein Leben*;
correspondence 81-3, see also
individual recipients; ensemble
music 46, e 125; operas and
scenarios, see individual works;
orchestral works 12, 15, 35,
53, 61, 62, e 111-12, e 113,
e 122-3, e 124, r 126, r 139,
r 140-42, see also individual
works; piano works 12, 30, 40,
e 113-14, e 123-4, r 142-3;
prose works 23, 31, 46, 53,
61, 68, 69, 75, b 76-9, 81,
85, 87, 88, 91, 93-4, 96, 99,
119, see also individual works;

songs and choral music 16, 17, 61, e 111, e 113, e 121-2, r 139, see also individual works
Wagner (Marbach), Rosalie (W's sister) 11, 13, 18, 110
Wagner, Siegfried (W's son) 10, 55, 56, 58, 69, 70, 107, r 136, r 138, r 141, r 142
Wagner, Wieland (W's grandson) 108, b 109
Wagner, Winifred (W's daughter-in-law) 109
Wagner, Wolf Siegfried (W's great-grandson) b 89
Wagner, Wolfgang (W's grandson) 108
Wahnfried 28, 59, 62, 63, 66, 68, 69, 71, 80, 81, 82, 85, 87, 88, 89, 92, 95, 102, 105
Walker, A D e 123
Walküre, Die 31, 32, 37, 43, 101, 113, e 118, e 124, r 131-2, r 136, r 137, r 138, r 140; conception and text 29, 33; composition of 31, 32, 33; in Karlsruhe 44; in Munich 56, 57; in Bayreuth 65-6; see also *Ring des Nibelungen, Der*
Wallace, W b 95
Warlock, P e 125
Watson, D b 97
Weber, C M von 10, 13, 21, 78, 111, 112, 121, 141; *Euryanthe* 13, 112, 124, 141; *Der Freischütz* 11
Weber, E von 69, 78
Weidmann (Stocker), Verena 37
Weimar 24, 26, 41, 48, 60, 61
Weingartner, F e 116
Weinlig, T 12
Wesendonck, Mathilde 29, 30, 33, 34, 35, 36, 37, 40, 41, 42, 44, 55, 57, 58, 62, 64, 66, 67, 91, 94, 113, 123, 142; W's letters to 45, b 83, 91

Wesendonck, Otto 29, 30, 33, 34, 35, 37, 38, 39, 40, 41, 42, 44, 47, 57, 58, 66; W's letters to b 83
Wesendonck songs 35, e111, e 112, e 113, e 115, e 121, e 122, e 123, e 125, r 137, r 139-40, r 141
Westernhagen C von b 92, b 102
Weston, J L b 99-100
What boots this knowledge? 70-71
What is German? 49, 61
Wibelungen, The 23, 78, 79
White, C b 96
Wieland der Schmied 25, 26, 62
Wigard, Professor 23
Wilde, O 87
Wilhelm I, German emperor 58, 61, 65, 66, 71
Wilhelm II, German emperor, 99
Wilhelmj, A 64, 93, e 125
Wille, Eliza 29, 34, 44, 45, 57, W's letters to 46, b 83
Wille, François 29, 45
Williamson, A b 101
Wilson, P C b 97-8
Winn, C b 105
Wittgenstein, Princess Caroline 24, 25, 31, 34, 60, 66, b 95
Wolf, Hugo 65
Wolf, Werner b 81
Wolfram von Eschenbach 21
Wolzogen, H von 68, 81, 83, b 85, b 105
Work and mission of my life, The 81
Würzburg 13, 25

Young Siegfried see *Junge Siegfried*

Zhukovsky, P 70
Zuckermann, E b 105
Zürich 25, 77, 80, 85, 94, 103, 113; W's residence in 25-36

154